To: LIZ

TESTIMONIES
for the Soul

Book 1

A book of mighty miracles
& mercy

Ron Knott & Tommy Thomas

TESTIMONIES
for the Soul
Book 1

Ron Knott & Tommy Thomas

River City Press, Inc.
Life Changing Books

TESTIMONIES FOR THE SOUL
Copyright 2007 Ron Knott & Tommy Thomas

ISBN: 1-934327-27-1
          978-1-934327-27-2

Library of Congress Control Number Filed For Acceptance.

Unless otherwise indicated, Bible quotations are taken from King James Version. Copyright 1982 by Zondervan Publishing House.

Graphic Design & Cover:
Sara Jo Johnson

Editors:
Latrice Thomas
Erika Pardee
Charlene Meadows

Publisher:
River City Press, Inc.
4301 Emerson Avenue North
Minneapolis, MN 55412
www.rivercitypress.net
publisher@rivercitypress.net

Acknowledgments

We acknowledge all those who so graciously gave their personal testimonies that are recorded in this book. As you will note some of the individual stories are very revealing. They tell the dark side of their lives while the devil was in control. But, they also give God the glory for their miraculous transformation. They overcame many obstacles and eagerly communicated their story to show others that they too can be set free.

Thanks for all the many hours of editing by Latrice Thomas and Erika Pardee. Your help was needed and appreciated.

I want to express my sincere thanks to my wife Sharon and daughter Kristi for sharing several computers and a host of supplies for this work.

And last, but not least, we thank the Lord Jesus for the many miracles He has performed for these and many others.

Contents

Introduction

They overcame him by the blood of the Lamb and by the word of their testimony… (Revelation 12:11 NIV).

The enclosed, real life stories are written in "first person" to publish miraculous events that have taken place in their lives. Most of these testimonies were taken from live interviews for the television show called "How to Beat the Odds," narrated by Tommy Thomas. Tommy has a weekly TV talk show on Sky Angel Christian television. He interviews folks who have an exciting testimony from all walks of life. As you will note in these stories, a divine power was the source that made the individuals' "mission-impossible" possible.

You will read in this book about many authentic miracles that our Lord and Savior performed for sinners and saints alike. Some say that miracles are over and God doesn't perform miracles in the New Testament Age. Here you will find legitimate miracles of healing: folks brought back from the dead, people attacked by demons, a prisoner set free who had a 125-year sentence, financial blessings considered impossible by Wall-Street, drug addicts set free, suicides prevented, one who returned from hell, and many more supernatural occurrences. God is God, and He is still in the miracle business!

These people are eager to share "their story" to help others change their lives and increase their faith. We may not see Christ in person today, but in these testimonies we can see Him through real life testimonies. God is no respecter of persons and desires all to be saved, healed, and delivered.

As recorded in the Bible (Revelation 12:11), our testimony is one of the most powerful tools that we have in witnessing for the Lord. No one can dispute an experience or a miracle performed by God. An argument can never override an experience. These stories are real!

You will note in these stories that God miraculously intervened so that these folks could have eternal life with Him. Mankind considers themselves human beings with a small spiritual experience, when, in fact, we are spiritual beings with a short human experience. We will be spiritual beings for billions of years and only human beings, 100 years, more or less. Nevertheless, what we do during our human experience will determine our spiritual address. Which experience should be in our long range planning?

What is eternity? The following example can only express the beginning of eternity. Say for example, that a drop of water out of an eyedropper is equivalent to 100 years of life. Therefore, the length of eternity could be represented by all the water, in all the oceans, seas, lakes, and rivers of the world. (How many drops of water representing 100 years would that be?) And that would only be the beginning of eternity! Which part of our existence should we be more concerned with, the human experience or the spiritual experience? Think about it!

Share Your Testimony

Please send us your "miracle" testimony. The testimonies chosen will be published in our next book. Please write your story in 3000 words or less. We will edit the article, then send it back to you for approval before it is published.

You can send your story to the address below or to my e-mail address.

Ron Knott
700 Knott Court
Euless, TX 76039
www.testimoniesforthesoul.com
ronknott1@msn.com

Tommy Thomas
www.howtobeattheodds.com
tommy2401@sbcglobal.net

Profits from the book will go to building God's Kingdom!

We know that you will enjoy reading our book of testimonies.

Ron Knott & Tommy Thomas

Miracle 1

Cindy
Raised from the Dead

Yea, though I walk through the valley of the shadow of death, I will fear no evil: for thou art with me; thy rod and thy staff they comfort me.
(Psalm 23:4)

"Cindy is dead," was the report that the doctor gave my family and friends. They were awaiting the results of my surgery in the hospital waiting room. Everyone knew something was gravely wrong as soon as the doctor walked in because of the dreadful look on his face. The doctor continued, "We tried everything but Cindy died just a few minutes ago. Her heart and lungs collapsed during the operation and we just could not revive her. I am sorry." He then departed the room as quick as he had entered, leaving my grieving family in a state of shock. A report such as this has got to be the most devastating announcement that a parent can hear.

I was the tenth patient to have this experimental surgery performed for my back problem. The other nine patients had died during surgery. I was told that if I elected not to have the operation, I would only live a few months. So I thought, "I might as well give it a try, it just might work." I was only twelve years old at that time.

The doctors pronounced me dead when my heart stopped beating and the monitors went straight line. But, I assure you, I was more alive than any other time, though my heart had stopped. I had an out-of-the-body experience and saw myself rising over the operating table looking back down at the hospital staff. They were desperately trying to bring me back to life. Finally, they gave up all efforts to revive me. They placed my dead body on a gurney to be sent to the morgue. Yet, my spirit departed the hospital and started floating through a tunnel toward a great light. At the end of the tunnel I came to a beautiful field with lovely green trees, grass, and beautiful flowers of all colors.

The golden light was so brilliant that it dominated everything else in the area. It was at least 10 times brighter than the sun; maybe a 100 times more brilliant than the sun. It was so bright that I could not look straight toward the source of the light. It was blinding. Yet, I started walking across the field toward the light. There was a stream at the edge of the field with a bridge going across the stream. I started walking across the bridge and noticed a man on the far end of the bridge reaching his hand out to me. I thought it was St. Peter since I was raised Catholic. I had heard all the stories about Peter being in control of those entering heaven. I heard the water flowing under the bridge announcing, "Holy, Holy, Holy is the Lord." This running water was the most amazing thing I had ever seen or heard. I had never been taught about the Living Water before. It was a babbling brook and it really spoke praises to God.

This Man, who was so radiant, held out His hand and said, "My child are you ready?" And I said, "No I'm not, I have not made a difference." He said, "It will be hard but you may go back." I said, "I need to go back and make a difference." I don't know why I said that, but the words just came up from within me.

The next thing I knew, I was waking up on the gurney in the hospital as they were rolling me to the morgue. My screams of pain got the attention of the hospital staff and they began working on me again. They had not placed stitches in my back, since they knew

I was dead and sutures were not necessary. The pain was dreadful as my life re-entered my body.

According to the medical report, I had been dead seven minutes. The doctors told my parents that I would have severe brain damage due to the lack of oxygen to my brain for such a long period. They said that I would never regain normal body functions, and that I would be in a vegetable condition the rest of my life. "Don't expect her to live very long if she recovers from the operation. She will die again very soon," the doctor said.

I was on life support for days. The hospital staff told my family that the chance of me improving enough to be removed from the life support apparatus was almost impossible. They recommended that my parents authorize them to remove my artificial life support. This was a very hard decision for my parents to make, but after considering the medical report my mother finally agreed to have it disconnected.

They waited for me to die. But the Lord had a better plan for me. I did not die as expected but got much better. Instead of having brain damage, I now had a photographic memory. I could read a book, then shut my eyes and tell you what was written on each page. Of course this was a miracle from God as well. I read all the books in the library and anything else I could get my hands on. I graduated early from high school and got a scholarship to college due to my scholastic abilities.

When I was in college, I was raped at age 17 and had a baby boy. I married the man who had raped me; which was a big mistake. My husband was very abusive. In fact, he would not allow me to visit my parents for over twenty-seven years. We were very successful in the furniture business, and had fourteen stores throughout the state of Texas. But we were very dysfunctional as a family. We went through family counseling, but that did not help our marriage. Thank God, they placed me with a Christian psychologist for counseling. During my session the psychologist would read the Bible to me. There was a little sign on the wall in the doctor's office that said, "And you shall know the Truth and the Truth shall set you free." This sign haunted me because I wanted to know the "TRUTH." I was desperate.

One night I laid out seven Bibles on the dining room table. I opened each Bible to a different book and chapter. Then I got down on my knees and prayed, "God I need to know the truth because you promised that the truth would set me free." Immediately the air conditioner vent came on and wind started blowing from the vent. The pages of the Bibles were going in many directions. The wind on the table was like a little tornado. After a few seconds the wind stopped and I noticed the strangest occurrence. All seven Bibles' pages were stopped on the same chapter and verse. Every Bible had stopped at Romans 10:9 which said, "If you confess with your mouth, Jesus is Lord, and believe in your heart that God raised him from the dead, you will be saved." I was astonished by this supernatural occurrence. God had answered my prayer by showing me His TRUTH in all seven Bibles. Then I obeyed that Scripture and a wonderful Spirit came over me. I hurried to the psychologist's office early the next morning to share what had happened. He was excited as well.

I read the Bible from cover to cover many times just to learn more truth. I started going to churches and finally was led to a Spirit-filled church. I was so hungry for the Word of God. I wanted everything that the Lord had for me. I was soon filled with the Holy Spirit and began speaking in tongues as recorded in the New Testament. What a joyful experience that was!

Our marriage went from bad to worse. My husband was impossible to work with. He wanted to control my every move and seemed to hate the ground I walked on. I was so very despondent. During this period of depression, a lady came by my store and left me a letter. She told one of my employees to give the letter to me and turned and walked out of the store. I was only about ten feet from the lady when she handed the letter to one of my employees. I hurried to speak with her and thank her for coming in as she departed. Just as she walked out of the store, she disappeared and could not be found. The sidewalk was empty, the parking lot was empty, and the lady just vanished. I hurried back in the store and read the letter. Here is what it said:

My Dear Child

I am writing to say how much I care for you and that I feel your pain. I have seen the tears that you have cried. I want you to know that I have been with you through your time of sorrow. I will heal your broken heart and care for your wounds. Let me be your strength.

Cast your cares upon me because I care for you. I have sent the comforter to you to build you up. When you pass through the waters, I will be with you; the rivers will not overflow you. When you walk through the fire you will not be burned. I want you to always remember that nothing will separate you from my love.

I have great plans for you and the gifts I have given you. Even though all others may fail you I will never fail you. I will be your shelter in the storm. Come to me and find rest and peace. I have made the sun to shine on you in the daytime and the moon at night. I have my hand on you and I will carry you through the dark storms. I will deliver you from all trouble. I love you, Jesus.

I cried and, of course, the letter was stained with many tears when I read it. The Lord knew that I was about to give up on life and He loved me enough to save me again from the troubles of this world. I knew that I now could get through the abuse or anything else because the Lord knew exactly where I was at all times and He was going to fight my battles.

My employees witnessed this lady coming into the store and vanishing. They all read the contents of the letter and knew that something miraculous had taken place. We got down on our knees at the front of the store and prayed. Many of my employees accepted Christ that day. They were all influenced by this awesome event.

Later on, my husband asked me if I would run for the "Miss Harley Davidson" contest that was soon to be held in our area. That request really worried me for a while. I was not about to take off most of my clothes in any beauty contest. I asked the Lord what He wanted me to do. He said, "Enter the contest." I was much older than the young beautiful girls that also entered. I knew that my chance of winning was not very good. In fact, I told the judges before the start of the contest that I would be fully clothed at all times during the event. They said that they only wanted me to improve the image of the Harley Davidson Company and the perception of the motorcycle riders. I told the judges that they could improve the image of the Harley as they ride by talking about Jesus.

I won the contest unanimously. This was a shock to the other contestants and myself as well. Later I found out that one of the judges was a member of the Banditos, a group which was considered to be an outlaw biker gang. What I didn't know was that a week before the contest I had prayed for his brother who was in prison where I ministered. His brother had accepted Jesus as his Savior as a result of my testimony. God really put it all together.

I sang a couple of songs for the group, and they were amazed at the quality of my voice. The Lord had anointed me as a child with a beautiful singing voice. When I was eight years old, we kids would sing as we played at school. My teacher heard me singing and said I had the voice of an adult at that age. She gave me free opera lessons for a long time and the Lord anointed my singing ability. This has given me the ability to sing for my Savior in prisons, churches and other places.

I was hired as a full-time prison Chaplain. All that I knew about faith was what I learned from the Bible. I just took God at His Word and believed what He said.

My first week as Chaplain, I was asked to pray for an inmate who could not hear and his speaking ability was very bad. I knew that I needed a miracle to demonstrate God's power to these prisoners. I prayed, "God please heal this man for a testimony so that others could see Your power." This division of the prison was known to have the most horrendous inmates and they were very disorderly. The bad guys were not about to let a female Chaplain get the upper hand with them and I knew that. I simply laid my hands on this big fellows ears and prayed, "I command you to hear and speak in Jesus' Name." He did. The prisoners went wild and so did I. Many inmates were saved that day. I had such an anointing on me that when I touched anyone they would fall out, slain in the Spirit. I was as shocked as the inmates were that this was happening. The funny part of this anointing was when the guards would come near me they too would fall out, slain in the Spirit. Of course I was instructed quickly to stay away from the guards!

My husband and I finally got a divorce. After 27 years, I was now able to go see my parents. My dad had a brain aneurysm and was in intensive care. We became very close before he died.

I am now married to a wonderful man. We have joined with our pastor to open homes for abused women, released prisoners and troubled youth.

Cindy

And we know that all things work together for good to them that love God, to them who are the called according to his purpose (Romans 8:28).

Ron

125-Year Prison Sentence: Cancelled

Because he hath set his love upon me, therefore will I deliver him….
(Psalm 91:14)

The Judge slammed the gavel on his bench and said, "Ron. I sentence you to an additional 25 years in prison. This will make your total time to serve in the Texas prison system 125 years." I knew I would never experience another free day in my life. I would be locked up until I died.

The reason for the additional 25-year sentence that was added on to my 100-year sentence was because I had broken out of jail in East Texas. Not only did I bust out, but I also took 3 pistols away from the Deputy Sheriff. This made the local law officials furious. I had planned to go out in a blaze of glory if and when they caught up with me. I was determined not to go back to jail. They launched a nation-wide manhunt for Ron. My name was in the news daily and I was considered armed and dangerous. I was able to escape and evade the law for 26 days, but they finally found me. There was no chance of me having a shoot-out with the cops, because they had me on the ground and handcuffed before I knew what was going on.

As a kid I was full of rebellion and enjoyed doing anything that was wrong. I got mixed up with the wrong crowd, got hooked on drugs, and was always breaking the law. My parents divorced when I was eleven and after that I just went wild. No one could control me and I did what I wanted to do, whenever, and wherever I wanted to do it. The Law finally caught up with me and I was sentenced to a total of 100 years in prison. The escape had added another 25 years.

Before I went to prison I had a beautiful wife and three small children that really loved me. But I didn't do much for them. I hated everybody and everything and didn't want love from anyone. I guess you can say that I enjoyed hate. The old devil really messed with my mind and tried to destroy me many times. I believe he was thrilled when I was awarded the 125-year sentence.

In prison my hate for everything grew stronger. I started having horrible nightmares. I would have a vision of being in a casket, buried alive underground, and unable to break out. I would kick and try to tear off the top of the casket. In the dream I would claw the top lining of the coffin trying to break free. I could not get free. Several times, after having the dream, my fingers would be hurting and bleeding from scratching the cell wall while I was hallucinating. This vision would appear every night, and nothing I did would stop this torment.

I went to the prison shrink for help and he prescribed anti-depressants to alleviate my agony every night. The medicine didn't help. Finally, they placed me in a straight-jacket and locked me in a padded cell. This confined cell was very small and lonely. I asked the guard for something to read, but this was not allowed. I cursed the guard, his family, and everyone else I could think of. Finally, after recovering from my fit of rage, I looked up at the small opening in the door and saw a little brown object. As I approached the door I determined that it was a small book. In fact it was a Gideon New Testament Bible. This made me mad because I sure didn't want a

Bible, especially now. But something strange came over me. I began to feel love and it felt weird and wonderful at the same time. I flipped the Bible open, from the back, and observed the words, "God loves you." Then I felt more love. I looked back at the opening where I found the Bible and there was a small penlight shining toward me. The light got much brighter until the entire cell was filled with its glow. Prior to this experience the cell was very cold, but now, I felt warm all over. I was bathed with unbelievable love for the first time in my life.

I read in the Bible that if I confessed the Lord, and believed that God had raised Him from the dead, I would be saved. I wanted that "saved" experience more than anything. I asked the Lord, "Would you please save me from my many sins?" Rivers of tears started flowing down my cheeks. Then I prayed, "Lord please make the dreams stop and silence the voices that have been tormenting me." I never had another bad dream after that prayer.

The doctor kept ordering the anti-depressant shots and I tried to tell them that God had healed me. "Of course," they said in a mocking tone, "yea, we know that God was in your cell." They also said, "A lot of prisoners get 'jailhouse religion' when things go bad for them." But later they finally saw a great change in me and gave me more freedom. I had been in prison more than fifteen years at this time.

I became friends with the prison chaplain. He helped me understand the Bible and the plan that God has for all of us. I was a new person, "born-again," and I felt very fortunate to be saved.

A few weeks after the salvation conversion I was delivered a small official letter during mail call. I had not received any mail in the last twelve years. In fact I had told my family not to write me. I hated everybody. So I was shocked that someone was sending me something. I opened the document and almost fainted. It was a pardon from the Texas Prison System. I thought, "Someone is playing a joke on me." But the document sure did look official. I took it to my chaplain friend and he said, "Ron, you will die in prison. Someone is pulling your leg." But he said, "Let me check just to be sure." After making a phone call he said, "Ron, you are going to be a free man in just a few weeks."

This was totally unbelievable. First of all, I had only served fifteen years of a 125-year sentence. Second, I was not eligible for parole. And third, I had not asked to be paroled. This had to be God or a terrible joke.

I really didn't get my hopes too high about leaving prison because I thought for sure that there was a big mistake of identity. "There was just no way this was going to happen," so I thought. I knew that the last thing they did before you left prison was to fingerprint you. This was what was going to stop me from walking out of that prison. But, after they fingerprinted me the warden said, "You are a free man."

When I departed the prison's main gate, I headed straight for the bus station. I still had doubts that I was actually supposed to be let out of prison and was somewhat nervous that they may bring me back. As I walked down the street a young man got in behind me and started walking in my direction. I would walk fast and he would walk faster, I would speed up and so would he. Then I knew they had me. The young man got closer and closer. He called out my name. My heart sank. He said it again. I turned toward him and said, "Who are you and what do you want?" He said, "Daddy, I love you and have come to take you home." This was my 21-year-old son whom I did not know. The last time we were together was when he was 6 years old. Of course, we both wept and had a great reunion.

That was the start of a new life for me over fifteen years ago. The Lord saved my soul, got me released from prison under the most impossible conditions, and restored my family. What an awesome God I serve.

My wife prayed for me the entire time that I was in prison. God answered her prayers. She and I are now passing out Gideon

Bibles in prisons, hospitals, schools, and hotels. I give my testimony in different churches almost every Sunday. Jesus is the answer to whatever we are going through, and I praise Him for it.

Ron

[EDITORS' NOTE: Jonah was delivered from the belly of the whale. The Hebrew children were delivered from the fiery furnace. Daniel was delivered from the lions' den. Paul and Silas were delivered from the local jail. And Ron Cummings was delivered from the Texas State Prison System. What a mighty God we serve!]

Miracle 3

Paul
To Hell and Back

…if I make my bed in hell, behold, thou art there. (Psalm 139:8)

I was in hell, real hell, with real fire. I could hear the horrifying screams and feel the tremendous heat on my body as I approached this detestable place. Flames were leaping thousands of feet in the air and seemed to enjoy the punishment that they were inflicting on the poor souls that had been sent there. People's bodies were burning like firewood, but the fire did not consume their flesh. The flames just seemed to stick to their bodies, but no matter how hard the people tried to shake off the fire it would not leave them. The stench was dreadful. All my senses were more alive than they had ever been. I could see hell; I could smell hell; I could breathe hell; I could hear hell; and I could feel hell.

My mother tried to warn me about hell, but I didn't want to listen to her old ways. I was a Communist teenager in Romania and we were taught in school that there was no God, no heaven, or hell. Mom pleaded with me to pray and read the Bible, but my Communist friends would say mockingly that only the weak would rely on such yarns. And besides this, it was against the law to believe in a God.

As I was being transported closer and closer to the inferno, I thought to myself, "I wonder what is Heaven like? How stupid I am.

I should have listened to mother. Now I see what she was trying to tell me but it's too late." My thoughts were somehow transmitted to a Young Man and He intercepted my route to hell. He rescued me on the one-yard line of hell and started me toward Heaven.

I was being sent to hell because I had just died from burns I had suffered all over my body and I was not saved. Mother had pleaded with me to go to church with her just once. I said, "I will go with you tonight Mom, but don't ever ask me to go again." She was thrilled that I was going at least once. That night we went into the little underground church and it was dark and cold. A few dim kerosene lamps provided the only light in the church. Bright lights would have attracted the KGB and they would beat and arrest the Christians if they found them worshiping.

Mom and I were the first ones in the church that night. I attempted to light one of the kerosene lamps so she wouldn't fall down the dark stairs. As I put the match to the lamp, it exploded in my face and burned over 90% of my body. It was a massive fire. The Communists had found the little church, and to teach the dumb Christians a lesson, they had placed gasoline in the lamps instead of kerosene.

They rushed me to the local hospital with very little hope of me living. I lay in the bed for several days, in intense pain, and then I died. And, as I stated before, I went to hell. But this Young Man intercepted my thoughts and directed me toward Heaven. While I was standing next to this Young Man I asked, "Who are you?" He said, "I am Jesus whom you have persecuted." Then he held out His hands and I could see the nail scars.

While I was there with Jesus, I could hear my mother praying for me in the morgue of the hospital. She said, "God, you told me when Paul was born that he was going to be an evangelist for You. Now the Communists have killed my son, but I believe that my God is more mighty than the entire Communist community and I know that you can bring Paul back." I was really impressed that my mother's prayer was amplified in Heaven just like she was standing next to Jesus. Yet, she was millions of miles away in the morgue room of the hospital where my dead body had been taken. Her prayer got the attention of Jesus. He gestured to a couple of angels nearby and they guided their hands over my burnt body. I was healed instantly. Then the Lord just nodded His head indicating that I would be returning to earth in response to my mother's prayer.

The next thing I knew was waking up in the morgue. I got up and started speaking in tongues, just like my mother had been doing for many years. I ran all over the place. The hospital attendants came running down the stairs where I was. They heard me speaking in tongues. They knew that I had been dead so they took off very frightened. The Lord had healed me completely. I still have the scars, like Jesus' scars in His hands, but I was completely made whole.

The Communist doctors were astonished and could not believe my recovery. In fact, they kept me in the hospital for several days and tried to get me to sign a document praising them for bringing me back to life. I would not sign anything and gave all the glory to my Savior.

Of course, I became a dedicated Christian after this and preached all over Romania. I was beaten, put in jail several times, but the more I was beat, the more people I was able to bring to Christ. Finally, a Christian group from England helped me and my family escape to England. Years later, after the Communist regime fell, I went back to Romania and started several churches with financial help from many American Christians.

The Lord had to get my attention the hard way. Now I am preaching all over the world about the love and power of Jesus Christ. Many of the KGB members and others, who punished me for being a Christian, while the Communists were in power, are now Christians. Thank God the wall has come down and we have an opportunity to witness for our Lord. No one needs to go to hell, not even your worst enemy. Please pray that the Lord will lead you to those who are about to enter eternity without knowing Christ.

Paul

Ron Knott
The Old Man and the Oil Wells

Give, and it shall be given unto you; good measure, pressed down, and shaken together, and running over, shall men give into your bosom….
(Luke 6:38)

The old man rode his wobbly bicycle to our church one cold Sunday morning. The wrinkles in his face looked like a crumpled road map. With his ruddy, leather-like skin, ruffled with deep wrinkles throughout, and his matted gray hair and beard, it was obvious that he had seen too many days in the hot sun. No teeth, either real or false, had rested on his gums for years. His clothes were tattered, dirty, and ill-fitting. Most would quickly identify him as a street person who had destroyed his well-being by a sinful lifestyle. That is, until you looked into his eyes. They presented a warm and loving man who just needed a little special attention. Bill's eyes related a story contrary to what his appearance portrayed.

When I saw him from a distance my first thought was, "Here is another bum wanting a handout." However, when the worship service got underway, Bill's countenance quickly changed from that of a tired old man to one with an angelic appearance. A heavenly glow enveloped his face. His warm smile and sincere worship revealed a deep, authentic, and fervent love for God. The intrinsic nature of his worship mesmerized me.

When church ended I introduced myself to the old man and soon learned that he did not expect a handout from the church folks. He only wanted to be blessed by his Savior, and from what I observed, he was truly blessed.

I asked, "Sir, is there anything that you need?" He simply replied, "My name is Bill." He gave me no last name, just Bill. Then he proceeded to tell me that he had seen angels all around the people in the church during the service. He said, "See that little girl over there? Every time she raised her hands to praise the Lord, angels rushed to her side and helped hold her arms up." That really got my attention, because the young lady he pointed out was the most dedicated and devoted young person in the church. Then he pointed out several other individuals around whom he had seen angels during the service. Bill's spiritual depth intrigued me. Someone or something was giving him authentic information to which others were apparently not attuned. I was eager to learn more from him and about him.

I asked him where he lived. He told me he lived in the middle of a cow pasture a few miles away from the city. I drove over there after church and was shocked when I saw the awful conditions of that place. His home was a camper shell for a pickup truck, which had been propped up on some old timbers so he could crawl under for shelter. That camper shell, his bicycle, and the clothes on his back were all he possessed. Wild animals had better accommodations than Bill.

Getting information out of Bill was impossible. He only wanted to talk about angels. Even so, I knew Bill was as sane as you or I. He was not mentally ill, unbalanced, or irrational. Angels seemed to be around him most of the time. Although I never saw one, I sensed the wonderful presence of peace every time I was with him.

Finally, I said, "Bill, will you let me rent you a nice, clean, warm place to stay?" I felt that is what Jesus would have done. It was not easy to persuade him, but he finally agreed. There was a mobile home park nearby that had a few homes available for rent. I rented a nice one for Bill and moved him in with his few belongings that very day. The following day I went by to see how he liked his new accommodations. I will never forget his response. He said, "I stayed in that tub for hours. The warm water felt so wonderful!" While thanking me over and over, he looked like a new person.

Winning the lottery could not have made me happier. For the first time in my life I experienced the truth of the saying, "It is more blessed to give than to receive." My heart was flooded with so much joy I felt that I could have floated to heaven.

I went to visit Bill the next day, but he was gone. The rental manager said she had not seen him since the previous day. I went back to the old cow pasture and he was not there either. I never saw Bill again.

That was several years ago. Did I entertain an angel unaware (Hebrews 13:2)? To this day I do not know. What I do know is that a short time later, my whole life turned around, as you will read in this testimony. I do not believe my life changed because I may have entertained an angel unaware. I believe it changed because of what God's Word says about taking care of the poor.

To me, giving God's way is an adventure. If I could have planned my life I would not have been able to predetermine a better one than I have experienced since I became a Christian. It all started with Bill. When I met him, I had only been a Christian a short time. At that period of my life I had lost all material possessions and was living in a Sunday school room, graciously loaned to me by my pastor. I said to myself, "This Jesus fellow sure has a keen sense of humor. Not only did He take my sins away, all my money is gone as well." Of course, joking about my loss was a coping mechanism for dealing with the devastation. I knew full well that I alone was at fault for my financial problems. I had started on a financial downward spiral long before I came to Jesus.

Soon after helping Bill my financial status began a drastic change for the good. A friend told me about an oil and gas company in Louisiana that was selling four storage gas wells. These wells had not produced any oil or gas for more than fifteen years. They were only used as underground storage reservoirs for stockpiling production from other wells in the area. When more gas was needed the company would just turn on a valve and let the storage gas flow into the nearby pipeline.

My friend worked for the company, and it was his job to keep the records of the amount of storage gas in the reservoir. He told me that his company was selling the surface equipment to the highest bidder. He said, "I know that there is about $25,000 worth of gas in those storage wells because I put it in them. Some company will buy the surface equipment not knowing of the stored gas and make extra money on the project. It will be a good deal for whoever buys it."

Neither of us had enough money to bid on this package. We contacted a local bank that agreed to lend us the necessary funds if we were the high bidders. We were shocked and a little apprehensive when we found out that we had submitted the high bid. This was a big venture and we were not quite sure how to proceed with the deal. Since I can attest that I knew absolutely nothing about oil and gas production, we solicited a Higher Power for directions. While we were asking for the Lord's guidance, the Lord brought Proverbs 3:9-10 to my remembrance: "Honor the LORD with your possessions, and with the firstfruits of all your increase; So your barns will be filled with plenty, and your vats will overflow with new wine" (NKJ).

Proverbs promised abundance if we honored the Lord. We took God's Word as a guarantee direct from heaven. It gave us the boldness and faith we needed to go ahead with the deal. We closed on the property and immediately pledged the first $25,000 from that project to the work of the Lord and helping the poor. We thought that $25,000 from the sale of the storage gas would be all the profit we would make; it would be our firstfruit.

The cost of drilling one gas well at that time was about $250,000 and that is with no guarantee of production. We bought the four wells ($1,000,000 value) for our bid of $50,000. All we had to do to start production was to open the four valves, one from each well, and let the gas and oil flow. This was the beginning of miracles for us in this venture.

In a short period we produced $25,000 worth of gas and paid the faith pledge as we had promised to do. A portion of the $25,000 went to the support of missionaries and the remainder went to feeding the poor.

Let me emphasize here that this pledge was an offering, not a tithe. It could not have been a tithe. Since we had no concept of how much money we were going to make, there was no way to know what one-tenth would have been.

We were sure, as was everyone who had any knowledge about these wells, that they would be depleted very quickly. To our amazement, however, they kept producing oil and gas! The local geologist said that his information indicated that there was no production in the area. Yet, our wells continued to produce.

Soon, other large oil companies leased land and drilled all around us, but they only hit dry holes. We were reminded of the story of the widow in the Bible who gave her last bit of substance to the man of God. She thought it was her last bit of goods, but the barrel continued to be replenished (1 Kings 17). We assumed that our wells would soon dry up, but they kept producing. Six months passed and the wells were still producing. Now we were making profit big time. We were able to give even more to the work of the Lord. The more we gave, the more the wells produced.

My partner and I now found ourselves in a real dilemma; all this extra money created an income tax problem. We incorporated our company and set up a retirement plan for our families to best utilize the extra income. We held board of directors meetings in Colorado, Hawaii and Europe.

Now, remember that our first pledge was not a tithe because we had no idea how much would be produced. Ten percent of nothing is nothing. Since nothing is all we had when we made the pledge, it could not have been a tithe. Our pledge was a faith offering. We were giving by faith based on Proverbs 3:9-10. Please note that this portion of Scripture is not part of the Law. First fruit giving is strictly giving because of our love for the Lord. It is a free-will offering for the sake of honoring God with our possessions.

One year passed and the gas wells were still producing. Five years passed and they continued to produce. Ten years later we were still getting a monthly check from these so-called "dry holes." The people familiar with the area knew the story. We told them and the geologist that God was directing the fruit of the ground (the oil) to us. Large oil companies in the area inquired about our procedures and methods to keep the production flowing. They thought we had some secret method of extracting petroleum from depleted oil wells. We did. Our "secret method" was found in God's Word!

Eleven years after this miracle started I received a call from the president of a large oil company inquiring about the possibility of purchasing our production. The wells continued to produce and we continued to give. By that time we had collected almost $2 million from those dry holes! (I wonder how long the widow's barrel kept producing?)

After checking with my CPA I learned that we should not sell the production for another eleven months for income tax reasons. I called the executive of the company and told him that we could accept a contract on the wells, but the closing date had to be eleven months later. He was pleased with the deal. Eleven months later he closed on the property for the same amount that we had originally paid. This large gas company, with many experts in petroleum production knew a lot more about the possibilities of these wells than either my partner or myself.

A few days after the purchase was completed I received another phone call from the president of the company who had bought the production. He said, "What did you do to make the wells produce? As soon as we bought the production from you the wells stopped producing." Needless to say I was embarrassed and told him that I would refund his money. He said, "No, we have investors who have covered the loss." Although I was willing to return the money, he indicated he did not feel cheated.

Many who observed this continuous miracle-in-play for eleven years and then witnessed the production die as soon as the ownership changed hands, agreed that God's fulfillment of the guarantee in His Word was the secret of this amazing success. Acts 10:1-4 talks about a man named Cornelius who was a devout man, generous, and devoted to God. He honored the Lord with his substance (he gave to the poor), and he was a man of prayer. An angel appeared to Cornelius and said, "Your prayers and your alms have come up for a memorial before God" (Acts 10:4, NKJ). This verse speaks of how highly God esteems giving to the poor. He will memorialize this type of generosity throughout eternity.

Now, the purpose of telling this story is not to say you will become an oil tycoon if you give to the poor. The purpose is to ask you a question. Would you rather give God's way and have your generosity become a memorial in heaven, or give man's way and build an earthly shrine?

The Lord will bless you as well. He does not honor individuals, He honors His Word! One of my favorite songs is "Thank You For Giving to the Lord," by Ray Boltz. That beautiful hymn tells of a man going to heaven and meeting those who he had played a part in their salvation. Just think of how we must feel if we have been selfish during this life and not help win the lost for Jesus. This thought was so vivid in my mind that I felt impressed to write the following lyrics for those who do not give to the Lord and His cause. I call it "The Non-Giver."

THE NON-GIVER

I DREAMED I WENT TO HEAVEN,
AND YOU WERE <u>NOT</u> WITH ME.
I WALKED UPON THE STREETS OF GOLD,
YOU WERE <u>NOT</u> THERE TO SEE.
I HEARD THE ANGELS <u>CRYING</u>
THEN SOMEONE CALLED YOUR NAME.
"HE IS <u>NOT</u> HERE," WAS THE REPLY THAT CAME.

THEN I HEARD MANY VOICES SAYING:

"SHAME YOU, FOR NOT GIVING TO THE LORD,
FOR WE ARE THE SOULS THAT WERE LOST.
SHAME YOU, FOR NOT GIVING TO THE LORD
HOW WE WISH YOU HAD PAID THE COST!"

OTHER VOICES SAID:

"I WENT TO YOUR SUNDAY SCHOOL
WHEN I WAS ONLY EIGHT.
BUT YOU SAID, 'I'LL NOT TEACH THAT LITTLE REPROBATE.'
I WANTED TO ASK JESUS INTO MY HEART,
YOU SAID, 'KID I DON'T HAVE TIME FOR YOU, YOU MUST DEPART.'"

SHAME YOU FOR NOT GIVING TO THE LORD!

"I WAS THE DRUNKARD OF YOUR TOWN,
AND BY THIS TERRIBLE DISEASE, I WAS BOUND.
YOU WOULD LAUGH AT ME LIKE A CLOWN,
AND THAT IS WHY YOUR JESUS, I NEVER FOUND."

SHAME YOU FOR NOT GIVING TO THE LORD!

"I WANTED TO GO TO YOUR CHURCH,
BUT MY SKIN WAS BLACK.
I DID GO ONCE, BUT YOU DIDN'T WANT ME BACK.
THIS IS A VERY SAD, BUT A TRUE FACT.
IN DISGUST I DIED OF AN OVERDOSE OF CRACK."

SHAME YOU FOR NOT GIVING TO THE LORD!

"YOU PASSED BY ME EVERY SUNDAY,
I WANTED AND NEEDED TO HEAR WHAT GOD HAD TO SAY.
IF YOU WOULD HAVE ONLY BEEN A GOOD SAMARITAN ON THE WAY,
THEN I WOULDN'T BE HEADED FOR DAMNATION TODAY."

SHAME YOU FOR NOT GIVING TO THE LORD!

"I WAS INFECTED AND DYING WITH HIV,
YOU DID NOT WANT ANY DEALINGS WITH THE LIKES OF ME!
IF YOU WERE THE CHRISTIAN YOU CLAIMED TO BE,
THEN I WOULD NOT BE LOST FOR ALL ETERNITY!"

SHAME YOU FOR NOT GIVING TO THE LORD!

"REMEMBER THE TIME,
A MISSIONARY CAME TO YOUR CHURCH,
AND YOU WOULDN'T GIVE A DIME.
YOU HAD A LOT OF MONEY
BUT WOULDN'T SEND ANY MY WAY,
AND THAT'S WHY I AM LOST TODAY!"

SHAME YOU FOR NOT GIVING TO THE LORD!

AND I KNOW UP IN HEAVEN,
YOU'RE NOT SUPPOSED TO CRY,
BUT I AM ALMOST SURE THERE WERE TEARS IN YOUR EYE,

JESUS CAME BEFORE YOU AND LOOKED YOU IN THE FACE,
HE SAID, "DEPART FROM ME, YOU SELFISH ONE,
YOU CANNOT ENTER INTO THIS PLACE."

SHAME YOU FOR NOT GIVING TO THE LORD!

Ron

Miracle 5

Della

Jailed 53 Times

…though your sins be as scarlet, they shall be as white as snow; though they be red like crimson, they shall be as wool. (Isaiah 1:18)

For thirty-one years, I lived with a needle in my arm taking methadone, heroin, and cocaine! I had nine different men in my life that were pimps. They kept me on the street selling my body. I was their property. Yet, they didn't care about me.

My family life was terrible. My mother was married four times and her husbands abused me physically and verbally. Needless to say, my home life was not good.

I was in jail fifty-three times and prison twice. I was in many self-help groups. I tried Zen Buddhism and everything else known to man to quit the drugs. I even prayed and cried out to God to help me quit but nothing worked.

Looking back on my life, I remember the first time I went into a church. I was nine years old. I didn't know what to expect at this Vacation Bible School. Maybe I would be beaten there as well. I had always been afraid of God all of my life. I didn't know anything about Him but I wanted to obey Him. The preacher said, "You're going to hell for your sins!" I didn't know what sin was. So I asked God to remove my sins and not let me go to hell. I didn't attend church after that because of the hate and abuse in my home. The situation at home went from bad to worse. I started smoking marijuana when I was thirteen. Soon I graduated to taking heroin just because I needed something to ease my mental abuse.

When I was in high school, I was in a terrible auto accident. A friend and I had been doing drugs most of the night and as we were driving home a drunk driver ran a red light and hit the side of our car. I was pronounced dead on arrival at the hospital. However, there was a special doctor on duty that night, and he ordered that I be given a CAT scan just to make sure that I was in fact, dead. In the scan, they found a very small amount of brain activity and quickly started procedures to bring me back to the living. This had to be a God thing because this was an unusual request by a doctor especially after a patient had been declared dead by another doctor.

I had seven skull fractures, brain concussions, many torn ligaments, broken bones, and I was in a deep coma. My mother was told that I would not live. After two or three days they said, "If this girl lives she will be a quadriplegic." Then my mother told the medical staff to take me off life support and let me die. They disconnected all life-support machines. But God had a better plan and kept me alive without artificial support.

After three months, I awoke from unconsciousness. The first memory I have after coming out of the coma was that of a doctor standing at the end of my bed. Looking down on me he said, "If you are ever able to get out of that bed you need to get on your knees and thank God because there is no medical way on earth you should be alive." I was soon discharged from the hospital and quickly forgot the many miracles that God had performed for me.

I married a heroin dealer because he told me he loved me. No one had ever told me that before and it sounded neat. This was the beginning of real trouble for me. Every day for two and a half years my husband beat me. No matter what I did for him, he still beat me. I was working three jobs just to support his habit. I had to get out of that relationship and determined the best way for me to make a living was prostitution. The prostitution profession was pure hell.

I finally got to the place where I said, "God, hell is better than this, so I am going to kill myself." I overdosed six times and should have died each time, but the Lord spared my life. Then I decided to walk in front of an 18-wheeler truck and end it all instantly. As I was about to step into the path of the fast-moving truck I saw a vision of heaven. It was so beautiful. I could see it, smell it, taste it and sense it. It was awesome! I just saw these curtains opened and could see there was a marble threshold and I heard a voice say, "Step through and live, or stay on that side and die." I don't remember making a move, but the next thing I knew was that I was standing in front of a big door and had my hand on the doorknob. I opened the door very cautiously and walked into the uninhabited building. I noticed that it was a church.

I had passed by this building many times in the past and never noticed that it was a church. I walked to the back of the church and saw another door and I opened it and went inside. I was overwhelmed because it was a Sunday school room. Immediately I fell on my knees, weeping and crying out to God to save me. "I am hopeless and need help. Please help me," I prayed. Then I heard a voice say, "I'll remove these desires." I had never heard that before. Never seen that, never read it, never thought it. I turned around and said, "Who the heck said that?" There was no one there except me. It was the Holy Spirit of God trying to get my attention.

I can honestly say when I got up off my knees I was changed! Miraculously changed, in less than five seconds, or whatever time it took me to get off my knees. I no longer was addicted. I no longer was dope sick. I no longer was despondent. I no longer was discouraged. I no longer was the same person!

I didn't have any material possessions, no home, no car, and no place to stay. "So now what do I do, God?" I asked.

He showed me a vision of 8th Avenue, and it was underlined in neon lights. The only thing I knew that I could acquaint with 8th

Avenue was an Alcoholics Anonymous club. I used to run and hide from the police there.

As I was walking there, a lady drove past me in her car. She noticed that I was alone and offered me a ride. When she learned of my condition, she helped me get a motel room, gave me bus fare and fed me for many days. I learned later of the "good shepherd" in the Bible and that is exactly what this lady did for me. I was really ashamed of my past and didn't fully realize that God had forgiven me, and He had washed and cleansed me as well.

Then the Lord began to convict me about some outstanding warrants and other violations on my police record, or "rap sheet" as it is known in street terms. I had a real fear about turning myself in because some charges could place me in prison for twenty-five years or longer. The Lord began speaking to me through the Scriptures. He showed me that He would be with me no matter what might be coming up in the future.

I told the Lord one day in prayer, "I can't do it. I'm afraid. I'm scared." I then looked up and the Lord appeared to me. He handed me His hand and He said, "Della, what's the right thing to do?" And I said, "Turn myself in, but I'm too afraid. I don't want to go back to prison. I'm sorry." The Lord said, "Take my Hand and I will walk you through this." When He said that, it changed my heart and I was not afraid any longer of any situation because I knew that He would be right with me.

When it came time for me to go to court I went without the aid of a lawyer. Jesus was my advocate. Eight ladies from my church came to court with me as my character witnesses. Each lady told the judge how she had seen a great change in my life and that I was really a new person who could be trusted.

My parole officer was not impressed with me or the testimonies from my friends. She recommended that I get the maximum sentence of twenty-five years behind bars. The state usually agrees with the parole officer but this time she was overruled. I was only given 6 months to serve in a nice prison (if there is such a thing). As God had promised, He was holding my hand again.

While I was in prison, a group of tough ex-motorcycle mommas, who now had a prison ministry, came into the unit to hold worship services. They asked if anyone wanted to be prayed for. I walked up to the bars of my cell and said, "Would you please pray for me?" As soon as the first lady laid her hands on my head, the Holy Spirit hit me so hard that it knocked me on my back. It was like a thousand volts of electricity surged through my body. It was the most wonderful feeling I had ever experienced. I got up speaking in tongues and praising my Savior. I had been baptized with the Holy Ghost with the evidence of speaking in tongues just like in the Bible. I felt like I was floating in the air. It was so marvelous!

Soon I was out of prison and found a good church family that helped me get my life back in order. Things have really changed in my family. My mother and I have a wonderful relationship and my twenty-seven year old son and I get along great. He would not speak to me for more than eighteen years. Now he checks on me everyday. God can, and does, change things.

It is so sad that most of the drug dealers that I knew are now dead. I buried over sixty friends who died in the drug lifestyle. God was really merciful to me.

Della

[1]Have mercy on me, O God, according to your unfailing love; according to your great compassion blot out my transgressions. [2]Wash away all my iniquity and cleanse me from my sin. [3]For I know my transgressions, and my sin is always before me. [4]Against you, you only, have I sinned and done what is evil in your sight, so that you are proved right when you speak and justified when you judge. [5]Surely I was sinful at birth, sinful from the time my mother conceived me. [6]Surely you desire truth in the inner parts; you teach me wisdom in the inmost place. [7]Cleanse me

with hyssop, and I will be clean; wash me, and I will be whiter than snow.
⁸Let me hear joy and gladness; let the bones you have crushed rejoice.
⁹Hide your face from my sins and blot out all my iniquity. ¹⁰Create in me
a pure heart, O God, and renew a steadfast spirit within me. ¹¹Do not
cast me from your presence or take your Holy Spirit from me. ¹²Restore
to me the joy of your salvation and grant me a willing spirit, to sustain
me. ¹³Then I will teach transgressors your ways, and sinners will turn
back to you. (Psalm 51:1-13 NIV)

Milton
Gang Leader

But where sin abounded, grace did much more abound.
(Romans 5:20)

"Son, you're going to be doing the same thing that I do, that is killing people." Those were the commands given to me by my earthly father when I was eight years old. As you will read in this testimony, I did all I could to obey dad's command until Jesus changed my life.

Hello, I am from Colombia, South America. I was a very miserable young man on my way to hell. But a beautiful lady handing out Bibles on the streets of Colombia gave me her testimony about Jesus. I was involved in drugs, alcohol, gangs, and was a hit man for the mafia.

I was involved in just about everything that was illegal. To name a few, I was good at breaking into cars, breaking into houses, and fighting in the streets. This all started when I was twelve years old.

My dad left home before I was born, when he found out that my mother was pregnant with me. Mom hated my dad so much that she tried to abort me several times. But the Lord didn't let that happen. My mother always told me that my dad had died before I was born. However, when I was eight years old, I was passing by a local bar and a man called to me and said, "I'm your father." I told him my mother said that my dad was dead. He said, "I know son, but believe me, you are my son, and I want you to be an assassin just like me." In fact, he pulled a gun out of his belt and took a bullet out of it and said, "Son, you're going to be doing the same thing I do, that is killing people."

He handed that bullet to me. I grabbed it in my hands as a treasure from my dad. I was proud that he was a killer and I wanted to be just like him. I remember this scene like it was yesterday, but I was only eight years old. A year later my dad was killed in a drug bust. He was a police officer, and also a drug dealer. He was working for the law and the crooks at the same time and his double life finally caught up with him. I wanted to be like dad and just maybe that would cause him to love me. I'll always remember his words, "You're going to be an assassin just like me."

I started working for the mafia as a hit man when I was in my teens. I was an "enforcer". When my boss was not paid, or someone took some of his merchandise, I would beat them up and let them know if they did not pay on time they would be eliminated.

That was my life and the money was good. I would take my friends to the bar and pay for all their drinks or whatever they wanted. I had a void that could never be filled. I kept trying all the wrong things in all the wrong places, but nothing seemed to bring me happiness. I had developed a terrible drinking habit. I was kicked out of three high schools for weapon possession, violence, and robbery. All this started when I was twelve years old, and I was a professional crook by the time I reached the age of sixteen.

Just after I reached the age of sixteen, I saw a beautiful blonde girl on the streets of Colombia giving out something to folks passing by. I learned later that she was with a missionary group from the states. This good-looking lady approached me and said she was a Christian. She had a book in her hand that I later learned was a Bible. She started talking about Jesus and invited me to a church service that night. I sure didn't want anything to do with a church or this Jesus fellow at that time in my life, but I really wanted to get to know this gorgeous blonde. Finally, I accepted her invitation just to impress her.

The church service was held in a big tent revival in our town. The blonde girl was excited that I came. She found me a chair in the front row. I would not sit down there because I thought it was a set-up for me to be shot in the back. That was how the gangs used to exterminate their enemy. They would set you in a chair and have someone in front of you talking with you while another gang member would slip up behind you and blow your brains out. So, I stood up in the very back of the tent where I could watch what was going on all around me.

Missionary Steve Hill from the states was the speaker at the church that night. He shared how God had changed his life when he was on drugs. He was so sincere telling his personal testimony that he cried. He looked back at me and said, "Jesus loves you, son and has a plan for your life." At that moment I began to cry for the first time in a long time. Something took a hold of my spirit and would not let go. I felt so ashamed. I had said years before that I would never cry again because my grandmother beat me so much when I was a kid. I finally made up my mind that I would never cry again no matter how much she hit me. But this night, I lost complete control of my emotions and was crying like a baby.

At the end of the service, Pastor Hill called for everyone to come up to the front of the tent for prayer. I would not budge. There was no way I was going up there with those people that I didn't know. And secondly, they were acting so strange, like jumping up and down and falling on the dirt floor. I thought to myself, "They must be on something very strong." Finally, I made a deal with God and said, "If that black man sitting near me goes down for prayer, so will I." I felt safe with my arrangement. From the looks of this guy he was not about to go forward. Would you believe he got up and went to the altar right after I made the deal with God? Then I had to go. Remember I am a gangster and looked the part with the long hair, beard, and earrings.

When I got near the front, Pastor Steve Hill jumped off the platform and greeted me. He asked my name. After that I don't remember what happened except I felt like a new person and was happier than I had ever been. (Later, I saw a video of the service and it showed me holding up my hands and praying to Jesus.) Just a few moments before, I was a gangster and hated everybody. Now I am crying and loved everybody. I surrendered to God that night and that proved to be the greatest decision of my life

The next day, I met with Pastor Steve Hill again. He said, "What's up?" I said, "All I know is that I have been crying all morning and I don't want anything to do with my past life." He said, "You've been 'born-again' and your old life is gone, erased, finished, and no longer has a hold on you."

Later that morning I saw a group of missionaries handing out tracts. I asked if I could help. They said yes and told me they were fasting for two weeks. I said, "What is fasting?" When they told me what it was I said, "Well I'm not going to eat for two weeks either."

They led me to a park in the main part of town. Pastor Hill was preaching to a group of teenagers who were not paying much attention to him. No one was responding to his preaching. Something came over me, and I ran to the people, in tears, shaking them and telling them, "You need to get saved! You need Jesus in your heart. Most of you know that I was a gangster and hated everybody, but last night Jesus came into my heart and changed me. I loved to hurt people but now I love people. The preacher is telling you the truth. You need this Jesus." Many came forward and gave their life to Jesus that day. This was the start of my evangelism. Pastor Hill was right on. The Lord did have a plan for my life in serving Him.

Pastor Steve Hill adopted me and brought me to the states. I attended Bible school at the Brownsville School of Ministry that was born out of the Pensacola Revival in Pensacola, Florida. There I met a beautiful lady and we are now married and have two beautiful children.

My wife and I have an awesome passion for souls. After Bible school I went back to Colombia and started a church there in the worst part of town among the gangsters, kidnappers, and drug dealers. It was hard for me to believe that I was once part of groups like that. The devil sure can blind a man's soul, but the Lord is eager to let His light shine in and expose the enemy.

I met with a group of dopers in Colombia who were in the same stuff that I was in at one time. I got on my knees in the middle of the street and said, "Guys I was once like you are. I hated everybody and everything, but Jesus came into my life and changed me. And He will do the same for you." I told them if they wanted to change their lives, "Just close your eyes, bow your heads, and ask Jesus to come into your heart." It is a rule that gangsters never close their eyes or bow to anyone. But that day they did and prayed the prayer of repentance. Many were saved that day.

In a short while our church grew to over 350 souls and most of then came off the streets of Colombia. Then we built three more churches in Colombia and some in Honduras as well. We also ministered in Guatemala and Cuba. Of course we preached all over the USA giving our testimony. I give God the credit for all He has allowed me to do. We planted a church in the south and are now back on the mission field.

Remember earlier in this testimony that a beautiful blonde was the one who first invited me to a church service in Colombia. I was saved at that service. While I was in Bible school, the Lord impressed me to contact this blonde lady and bring her up-to-date about what He was doing in my life. I was finally able to make contact with her after searching for her phone number for days. I just wanted to let her know what the Lord had done in my life as a result of her witnessing to me. When I introduced myself on the phone, she began to cry. "Milton, I backslid," she said. This time I was able to lead her back to the Lord. The old saying of "what goes around comes around" was true in this situation.

My testimony is proof of God's love for mankind. Never, never, never think that someone is too sinful for God to save. That is the very one He came and died for.

Milton

Tammy
Alcohol and Drug Addiction

But if our gospel be hid, it is hid to them that are lost.
(2 Corinthians 4:3)

I was raised in the home of my wonderful parents, who were quite wealthy. We had everything we needed, but there was still a major void in my life. I had no conception what was missing in my life. I was extremely shy and had a fear of people. The only way I knew to overcome this shyness was to use alcohol and drugs. Of course that was a fabrication on my part, but I felt it helped me to be more outgoing and accepted.

After I ran away from home the fourth time, my dad moved my brother and I to Lubbock, Texas to operate one of his video stores. My parents were pretty much tired of the way I was acting. I was rebellious to authority. In fact, I had been arrested several times for breaking the law. I was searching for something, but I did not know what?

One Halloween night, a young man dressed in a cowboy costume walked into the video store. I was dressed in a little red devil costume that really fit my character. This cowboy had been to a church function that evening. After we talked for a while he asked me for a date. I said, "No!" He appeared to be a "goody two -shoes" type and I didn't want to be caught dead with him. I knew he didn't drink or do drugs so I was not interested in him. However, a friend of mine suggested that I go out with him since he was so persistent.

On our first date we went to a restaurant and he actually prayed for the meal in front of all those people! I was mortified to say the least. Then he introduced me to many of the youth from his church, they wore pins that said, "I love Jesus". That was too much for me to handle. After the date I told my mother that I would never go out with him again.

This same Christian guy, Britt, applied for a job at our video store and my brother and I decided to hire him. (Unbeknownst to me he had his own contracting business.) After being around him for a few days at work, I noticed that he was filled with joy and contentment. He was enjoying life and did not have to do drugs to be happy. He just loved Jesus.

I asked him many questions about his happiness. He would say, "Jesus makes me happy." He also told me about heaven and hell as recorded in the Bible. This really got my attention. I knew that I was headed to the wrong place.

I was falling in love with Britt and my Savior Jesus Christ at the same time. Britt and I had planned a dinner date, and then I was going to pray to receive Christ afterwards. The Lord had other plans. While I was in the shower getting ready for the dinner date I said, "Lord I really want you to come into my heart, but we must wait for Britt." The Lord didn't wait. I felt the Holy Spirit fill me instantly. I had never felt such joy and peace.

Six months later, Britt and I were married. I quit taking drugs and smoking cigarettes, but the alcohol addiction hung on. Alcohol really had a strong hold on my life. I could not break the addiction no matter how hard I tried.

After a short while my marriage started falling apart due to my alcohol problem. I started going out with my friends, partying and drinking even more. I didn't want to be around Britt anymore because he was a non-drinker. I came to the conclusion I needed to move out of our home.

My mom said, "You know you don't want to do this. You've got two small children who need both of you. You must stick it out and besides this, you love Britt." She encouraged me to stay with him and she was right!

After much thought and prayer, I made a decision in my heart that I was going to stay with Britt no matter what! I told the Lord, "I'm going to stay with this man even if I'm miserable." I thought I would be very uncomfortable in the marriage but this was just another lie from the devil.

I am so glad that I came back home. Britt and I decided to get back in the Word and in church. We had both drifted from the Lord. I had wasted ten years drinking and doing my own thing when I should have been following the Lord. The devil did not want me to know about the wonderful life that Jesus had for us.

We both committed to read the Word daily. When I was reading the Bible, I would feel such extreme conviction. I wanted to quit drinking so very bad, but I just had to have another drink, which led to another, and another. I would usually hold out until 5 o'clock in the afternoon, and then I would start drinking again.

I prayed, and prayed, and prayed about this drinking problem but I could not shake it. Britt and I had dinner at a local restaurant where I usually consumed three glasses of wine. I only got two glasses this particular night and it just made me want more liquor. I knew that my liquor pantry at home was empty so I pleaded with Britt on the way home, to stop at the local liquor store. He stopped as I requested. Then, this feeling of madness came all over me. I was angry with myself for not being able to quit drinking. I said, "Lord I don't want this anymore, I am tired of being addicted to alcohol."

The Lord delivered me from alcohol at that moment. I did not buy booze that day, nor have I had another drink since. God's Word finally healed me from my alcohol addiction, but I had to completely let go of it first, and trust Him completely with the outcome.

The devil tries to make us humans feel unsure about ourselves and to feel insecure as well. Some folks will try to hide that insecurity with dope or alcohol. That is what I did and it was a trap. I did cocaine and speed and all that stuff for ten or twelve years. It's easy to get caught up in that type of pitfall. But God doesn't want us in a trap set by the devil. He knows that is just a trick to destroy the plan that He has for our lives.

When I surrendered to God and said, "Okay, Lord, whatever you want; your will be done, and not my own." He immediately took hold of my life and sent me on a great adventure for Him! I knew nothing about the ministry He had planned just for me, but He taught me everything I needed to know about it. I knew nothing about drama, dance, or filmmaking. I didn't even know I was capable of doing these things. But God, slowly and graciously, showed me how to work for Him in each of these areas.

Now I know what God had planned for me and my husband to do. Our purpose is to loose the chains of injustice, untie the cords of the yoke, and set the oppressed free by creating unique workshop experiences that exalt God. We long for people to experience God through worship and the arts including film, song, dance, drama, and sign language.

As I move forward in this ministry, my husband is my support, my helper, and my knight in shining armor. He helps guide me on this great adventure that God has us on.

Tammy

Tommy Thomas
The Gambler

He shall call upon me, and I will answer him: I will be with him in trouble; I will deliver him, and honour him. (Psalm 91:15)

My dad had divorced my mother when I was two years old. I grew up reading about him in Life magazine, Golf Digest and Sports Illustrated. I wanted him to love me and felt the best way to do that was to become a professional gambler like him. I started practicing with a deck of cards and a pistol when I was thirteen.

When I was nineteen a good friend, Mike, knocked on my apartment door and asked me if I knew Jesus. I said, "I don't think I do." Mike invited me to the local Baptist church. I went wearing wrap-around sun glasses and would not take them off because of the tears flowing from my eyes because of the love I felt. I was baptized that night and was so excited. The next day I didn't know what to do and that is exactly what I did—nothing!

I went to Texas looking for my dad. I found him in San Antonio hitting golf balls in front of his house. As I walked toward him he said, "Who are you?" I said, "I am your son and I've come to live with you." "What do you do?" He asked. "I'm a gambler…just like you."

(I had been cheating at cards in the local Elks Club and thought I knew it all.) He smiled and said, "Do you have any money?"

"Yes sir, about four hundred dollars." At that time dad was seventy-one years old and married to his fifth wife who was twenty-six. He beat me playing poker, pitch, and gin rummy. Each time he would give back my four hundred dollars.

Dad and I spent a lot of time together over the next few months. We would go to poker games, the golf course, and bowling alleys. The best card cheaters in the world would come to see dad and I would spend hours mastering what they taught me. Dad told me I was the best he had ever seen with a deck of cards, but he never told me he loved me. My dad was finally proud of me. The last time I saw him was in the nursing home and he was very sick. I was leaving for a high stakes poker game out of town. He said, "Son, I guess I am going to die here." Then he put his arms around me and said, "I love you, son." I had been waiting my whole life to hear those words. Dad died while I was away playing poker.

After divorcing my step-dad, mother moved to Texas and continued to have a serious problem with alcohol. It was determined that she had throat cancer due to years of smoking. I prayed every night for God to bring us closer together before she died.

Five months before she died, I had a dream in the early morning hours. In the dream I was a young boy again in the days of Jesus. I was playing in the woods, like I used to when I was a boy, when all of a sudden I came upon a clearing. Looking across the clearing I saw a man with a robe standing on a hill talking to a lot of people. It got dark, and I was afraid and lost, and I didn't know the way home.

I went to the hospital to see my mother. I asked her if she knew Jesus and she said, "Of course, son, I know Jesus." We held each other and cried. My mother told me how much she loved me. I had not heard those words since I was a young boy. Mother died a few months later on Mother's Day eve.

In 1995, four weeks before Easter, I took a look at myself in the mirror and didn't like what I saw. I said, "God, I have been taking from people all my life. When I die, I want someone to remember me for giving instead of taking." I fell down on my knees and cried out to Him.

Two weeks later, I was waiting for my turn in a barbershop when I met a Christian lady named Margaret Moberly. Even though we had never met before, she knew everything about me. She said that God had told her, "That man is a professional gambler. He has a lot of nice things, but he isn't happy. He has a big heart, and God has him on a long leash."

I was blown away. I responded, "Lady, it doesn't get any better than being on a long leash with God, does it?" She didn't laugh. The night before Easter, she sent me another message through a friend, "Tell him that God now has him on a short leash. The devil has made a bet on his soul, and God has covered the bet." God really had my attention then. I said, "Where do you go to church? I will be there."

That Easter I went to church with Margaret. Again, prompted by the Lord, she said, "Tommy, when you were a teenager, God called you to be an evangelist and everything in your life has led up to that end." When she said those words, I felt like someone poured hot oil in me. She said, "Look at his face, can you see the difference?" I have never been the same since. I knew then there were only two winning hands, and they were nailed to the cross for me.

For the next several months God would wake me up in the middle of the night and remind me of all He had done for me.

He began to put my testimony together. For months, every night, I would wake up—going over what God would bring to my memory.

A friend who had a Harley Davidson motorcycle, like mine, invited me to his dad's church service. His dad was a Pentecostal preacher. When we arrived they asked me if I had ever been baptized in the Holy Spirit. I really didn't understand what they were talking about and didn't want anything to do with it. However, after the second visit to that church, I was invited to go up front and be prayed for. Men laid their hands on me and prayed that I would receive the Holy Spirit. I kept my eyes shut and knew nothing was going to happen; they were just wasting their time.

A man, who I didn't know, walked up to me and whispered in my ear, "I had a dream last night about a man on a Harley and God told me He was going to use this man, and that I was supposed to tell him about the dream. I knew when I saw you ride up, that you were that man." All of a sudden sounds that I did not know came bubbling out of my spirit. I was speaking in tongues, the evidence of receiving the Holy Ghost. I felt like I was supercharged with a thousand volts of energy. I had never experienced anything like that in my life. Instantly, I went to a new level in God. I didn't know it was possible to love God that much and all I wanted to do was tell people about Jesus Christ.

Not long after receiving the Holy Ghost I was invited to go to a prison for a worship service. There were over one hundred prisoners in attendance that day. I had made up my mind that I was not going to say a word. I just wanted to watch and listen to the service, but I was invited to speak. Then I cut a deal with God. (How stupid of me cutting a deal with the creator of the universe.) Nonetheless, I said, "God, if you can show me that what I am about to do will make a difference to these men, I will take your Word into the streets, jails, prisons, churches, and anywhere else you want me to go. I will follow you all the days of my life."

As I began to share what God had given me so many times in the middle of the night, something happened! It was like it was no longer me who was speaking. Tears were running down my face and it didn't make any difference. When I finished all the men jumped up and ran forward. One man said, "I rode a Harley in a gang and now I want to ride for Jesus." Another said, "I am getting out next week. Where do you go to church?" They all wanted prayer. They encouraged me and thanked me for being there.

Since that day I have kept my end of the bargain I made with God. And He has kept His.

I am now a volunteer chaplain and have preached the gospel in maximum security prisons for the last twelve years. I also have a weekly TV program on "Sky Angel Christian Satellite" called "How to Beat the Odds." We witness to millions each week.

I am so thankful that God never gave up on me. He has given me the love that I was looking for and given me a new purpose in life. I know that God loves me, not because of my ability or performance, but because He is my Father, and I am His child.

Tommy Thomas

[EDITORS' NOTE: For more of Tommy's testimony, please check his web page: www.howtobeattheodds.com]

Terry
Tormented by Demons

Then goeth he, and taketh with himself seven other spirits more wicked than himself, and they enter in and dwell there. (Matthew 12:45)

I was sitting on my couch when all of a sudden I noticed demons pressing against my outside windows trying to enter the house. I could see them as well as I have ever seen any person. They were saying to me that my lady friend and her daughter had just died. This lady and her daughter were my best friends and I loved them dearly. The demons knew how to get my attention by using my loved ones as a trap to get my focus.

I basically told the demons that they were welcome into my life, and could use my place as a haven if they would leave my girlfriend and her daughter alone. And from that moment on, for the next three to four weeks, I had physical manifestations of demons that were unbelievable. Other folks who were in my home saw the demons as well, so this was not just my imagination.

When I would turn a light on, the demons would say, "We hate the light, turn it off!"

I could feel them physically pushing against my body. I also saw my dead grandmother in one of my beds. Another time I woke up and saw my own deceased mother lying next to me. One night a demon emerged looking like a hairy beast and tried to kiss me. I told folks these evil spirits are real. They were as real as you are reading this testimony. I will write more about the demons later in this report but first I want to let you know how I got into this predicament.

As a teenager in high school I was very popular and was elected class president of my high school. After high school I went to college on a football scholarship. Again, I was very popular and made the dean's list for scholastic achievement. After graduating from college I landed a good job and was elevated to the top of that company very soon. I fell in love with a girl in college and we got married. It was a wonderful marriage.

Soon after college I got addicted to bodybuilding and started using steroids. I would do anything to make my body look good. I suppose my body was my idol. I quickly developed and advanced to 3rd place in the "Mr. Texas" competition for bodybuilders. Needless to say I really got hung up on myself and pride was all over me. Because of my pride I started being unfaithful in my marriage.

It wasn't long until my life started on a downward spiral. My wife divorced me for being untrustworthy and, about the same time, I severely injured my back. This really caused me an enormous amount of depression and sorrow. Not only had I lost my wife, but I had also lost my ability to lift weights as well. I could not maintain my idol, which was my physique. This caused a lot of pain, which led me to taking painkillers, which led to getting hooked on many illegal drugs. Taking drugs led me into selling drugs to help pay for my habit. I had many relationships with the ladies during the drug days and several of them became pregnant. I hate to tell you this but I devastated a lot of girls' lives by suggesting that they have an abortion. I paid for their terrible operations just to get rid of them.

Needless to say the old devil had a spiritual stronghold on me and did everything he could to destroy Terry. For example, at noon one beautiful cloudless day I was sitting in my living room, and all of a sudden a dark cloud came over the top of my room. Then a demon about twelve feet tall appeared and said, "I'm coming to kill you tonight because of the evil that you have done in your life." I was really frightened. The only thing I knew to do was to pick up a Bible and I began to read. I read until six o'clock in the evening. After laying the Bible down the demon reappeared but this time a cloudy mist came into my home. It covered the floor and was about three feet deep. This sight reminded me of a scene from a horror movie. There was a coldness in the house that I can't explain.

I could hear the old accuser saying all these evil things about me. He said, "You have hurt a lot of people. You have caused numerous abortions." As he talked I could feel the pages of my Bible turning wet as I tried to reopen it. I said, "Devil, you are a liar." And he left. But he kept coming back over the next three weeks. He convinced me that if I killed myself he would not hurt any of my loved ones or friends. But he said that if I didn't kill myself he would destroy all those I loved. I bought into that lie and planned to commit suicide that night.

I was lying on the floor with a pillow folded under my head. I had my 9mm revolver, fully loaded in my hand, ready to end it all. I placed the pistol to my temple and pulled the trigger, but for some reason the gun snapped and did not discharge the round. Later I inspected the cartridge and found that it had an indention where the firing pin had struck it with enough force to fire the round but something mightier than the devil stopped that bullet from killing me and sending my soul to hell forever. Of course I know now that the Lord had stepped in and saved my life once again.

I ran out of the house as fast as I could thinking that the house was the problem. There was a small group of children playing in the yard next door and the devil said, "If you don't fall on the metal stake sticking out of the ground and kill yourself I will surely kill all those kids." I thought about all the abortions that I was involved with and did not want any more kids hurt because of my sins and selfishness. I jumped up and landed on this sharp spike with all my weight. The spike penetrated my body and went into my chest cavity about four inches. The amazing part of this story is that I did not bleed a drop. None of my vital organs had been damaged.

I went to the hospital to get the large wound treated. After the doctor examined my chest he said, "We need to have surgery to repair this large laceration." As I was recovering from the surgery the demons again tried to kill me. They told me that if I would only jump out of the window on the seventh floor of the hospital they would not hurt any of my friends or family.

About that time one of my friends entered the hospital room. The devil told me that if I told my friend that he wanted me to jump out of the window that he would kill him. So I told my friend to leave the room. He did, but later told me that he could feel the demonic spirits all around the room.

Then I heard a soothing voice whisper this message to me, "They can't hurt you." I knew instantly that it was the voice of Jesus.

Within minutes folks from a local church came in and gave me a Gideon Bible. When I started to read, the demons fled. This is when I turned my life over to Jesus.

When I was released from the hospital and returned home the demons again tried to attack me. But I just read my Bible and rebuked them in the Name of Jesus and they fled. I got on my knees and asked the Lord to get rid of those evil spirits once and for all. I also asked Him to heal my damaged back. When I asked the Lord to heal me I had a warm feeling all over my body and it felt like a cross was lying on top of me. God accomplished both miracles with ease. I haven't taken medication in years. All the pain departed that day, never to return. I have not had another visitation from the evil ones in years and my back is completely healed.

I am now in a great church, teaching Sunday School, and love serving others. The devil tried to destroy me but the Lord healed me spiritually and physically.

Terry

Sam Evans
What is Success?

For what shall it profit a man, if he shall gain the whole world, and lose his own soul? (Mark 8:36)

I was known as the "franchise king," with a net worth over $70 million. I lived in a 14,000 square-foot house on 1000 acres of land with my Learjet waiting outside. I was living it up, but I was on a merry-go-round that seemed to be moving faster and faster and faster….

My law firm was skilled in directing the overall operations for diversified-type entities up to $100 million. I was associated with Michael Landon and Loren Green as principals in the Bonanza Steakhouses. The company merged with Ponderosa, to become the world's largest steakhouse chain. I had graduated from one of the top law schools in the nation. I was a member of the U.S. Senate Advisory Committee and U.S. Presidential Task Force. But something was missing in my life and I didn't have a clue what it was.

I was on many business trips around the world and did not spend much time with my family. I remember well a return flight from Japan when a feeling of guilt came over me. In my way of thinking I reasoned that I had my own Learjet, and my wife and fourteen year old son did not have one. So in my carnal way of reasoning, to rid myself of this guilt, I ordered two more Learjets for them.

I had hired an outside accountant to do some work for me at my Dallas office. In one of our conversations, he said, "Hey Sam, if you are ever in Atlanta be sure to visit my church, the Mt. Paran Church of God." "Sure," I said, but couldn't help but think that it was a peculiar thing to say to me. To begin with, I wasn't much of a church-goer, and then, even when I got to Atlanta, I never stayed longer than it would take for me to close a business deal.

In truth, I never seemed to stay anywhere for long, even in the dream house outside of Dallas where my wife, Patty and our three children lived. I hadn't settled down since the day I ran away from home when I was fourteen and signed on with a freighter. I had a burning desire to become the ship's captain. I soon learned that you aren't captain of anything without an education, so I worked my way through law school at night, and then began working eighteen-hour days. I became a very successful lawyer.

On the way home from a business trip to England, I shuffled through the Atlanta airport to connect with my Dallas flight. I was bone-weary. Patty's plea for me was to spend more time with her than putting deals together. I was getting tired of hearing myself say, "I'll bring something nice back to you."

Just before the check-in counter, I noticed two young women standing in the corridor holding books. Before I could skirt around them, one pushed a Bible into my hand. I stopped. "Why in the world are you out here handing out Bibles in the dead of the night?" I asked. They both looked at me and smiled.

"We're doing it because of love," one said. "Because Jesus loves you." I simply could not think of a reply.

As I turned to leave, the other said, "Come visit our church sometime. It's the Mt. Paran Church of God." My mouth must have fallen open. In less than two weeks I had been urged to visit that same church. This seemed odd.

Shortly after that night my merry-go-round broke down. We hit the recession of the 70's and suddenly my empire began to crumble. I seemed to lose everything overnight. I sold our home and invested the money in another venture, but, unbelievably, before long I lost that also.

About all I had left was the patent and rights to market an anti-shoplifting system that had been developed in Atlanta. Almost broke, I went out on a limb and moved my family there, persuading my secretary, Sue Borah, to come along and help us make the transition.

One day, out of the blue, Sue said, "You know I've found this wonderful church here. The Mt. Paran Church of God…."

"I might have known it!" I said. "I'd like to meet someone in Atlanta who doesn't go to the Mt. Paran Church of God." "How is that?" Sue asked, puzzled. "Never mind, let's get back to work," I said.

Not long after that Sue had to return to Dallas, and I asked an employment agency to send some secretaries for me to interview. I sensed immediately that the first candidate was very capable. I decided to hire her on the spot. Then, after we had discussed her responsibilities, she exclaimed, "By the way, I'd like very much for you and your family to visit my church."

A funny tingling ran down the back of my neck. "And," I managed with a smile, "would that most likely be the Mt. Paran Church of God?" "Why, yes!" she smiled, quite surprised. "How did you know?" I could only shake my head. There it was again.

I dove into the businesses with my same old fiery determination, but I couldn't seem to get the company off the ground. Meantime, we were buying a home from an Atlanta lawyer. Patty and I were chatting with his wife in their kitchen. After a bit of small talk, she suddenly said, "If you're new in our community, Mr. Evans, perhaps you'd like to know about our wonderful church…."

"Oh no!"

"You really ought to come. It's the Mt. Paran Church of God."

This time I wasn't even surprised. Something inside me seemed to give way, and I decided right there, in that sunny kitchen, yes, I really ought to go to the Mt. Paran Church of God.

The next day Patty and I slipped into the balcony of the huge 7000-member church located just north of Atlanta. As we entered the church we were shocked to say the least. We thought these people were some kind of a cult. They were raising their hands and talking in other languages, but they all seemed so happy.

As soon as the minister said the opening prayer I knew that I was riveted. I sang the hymns as if I had sung them many times before; they seemed familiar. When the minister started preaching, he spoke to me, to the core of me, peeling away the protective layers of my old, hard-nosed business self.

"Are you alright, Sam?" Patty asked, for I was trembling. I nodded yes, noticing her eyes were shining too. Part of me wanted to bolt, part of me never wanted to leave the sanctuary. I knew that in some inexplicable way I was meeting God. I knew that He was what I had been searching for all my life.

"Lord Jesus," I whispered. "Forgive me. Help me."

Patty's hand tightened around mine. I scarcely remember the rest of the service, only that I was being touched in the empty places deep in my soul.

Patty and I returned to Mt. Paran that evening with our children, and every Sunday after that. Remarkable things began to happen inside me. The awful driving spirit, my insatiable need for wealth, power and success disappeared. It was as if from the moment I walked into that church, God began to crumble the flimsy foundation I'd built my life on. I came to relate to God in a personal way; to talk with Him…know Him!

The experience made me want to work full-time for God, so Patty and I asked the pastor and his wife to join us for dinner. Dr.

Walker, the pastor, listened intently when I blurted, "I want to do God's work!"

Dr. Walker gazed into my eyes as if he knew exactly what I was thinking; that God's work was church work, and running a business was something else.

"You're a businessman Sam," he said. "There are opportunities there to do God's work you've never dreamed of. Make your business God's business." He was right! I walked out of that restaurant with a new vision.

Meanwhile, the new company I'd been having such a struggle with turned completely around. I soon sold the business and moved to Cleveland, Tennessee, where the general offices of the Church of God are located. It is here that I founded "American Safety Products." This company now makes fire extinguishers that are sold worldwide. Now, my wife and children work with me, helping run the business.

Today our company is one big family. We've been able to give a good percentage of our profits to God's work. One year at our sales meeting we even had a prayer service, and during the altar call 31 people opened their lives to God.

As I stood in that crowd of smiling faces, watching those people give themselves to Him; I had to think back to the wreck I'd been only a few years before! In a very short time I had discovered that real success and real fullness in life comes not from what I can do for myself, but what I can do for God, and others, in His name.

My son and I were on a business trip to Bermuda and we noticed that there were motor scooters for rent. We wanted to zip around the island like many others were doing so we rented a pair of the little monsters. I soon crashed mine and broke seven ribs. The pain was dreadful. The medical staff told me that I must stay in bed at least two weeks to keep from puncturing my lungs. They told me that it was out of the question for me to fly back home until the ribs had time to partially heal.

The second day, after my injury, the maid came in my room and told me I had to get up so she could make my bed. I told her I could not get up due to my broken ribs. It just so happened that I was reading the Gideon Bible about divine healing. The maid asked me if I believed what I was reading. I said, "Of course!" Then she said why don't you get up if you believe that God can heal you. I thought to myself, "This lady does not understand how much I am hurting." I eased over to the edge of the bed, experiencing great pain, and stood up. As soon as I stood up the Lord completely healed my seven broken ribs. I was on the next airplane home.

I was elected the International Chairman of Full Gospel Business Men and traveled to many countries with that fine organization. On one trip to Africa I caught a deadly virus that caused me to have a heart failure. I was in the hospital for almost two weeks with no improvement. Finally, I called back to the states to find the nearest location of a Bible-believing church. I told my wife Patty, "Bring me my clothes, I am getting out of here and we're going to church." We walked into the church after it had started and the Pastor stopped his sermon and said, "Someone here has a serious heart problem. If they will come forward God will heal them." Patty said, "Sam, that is for you." I went forward and was healed instantly.

During my travels, to many countries with FGBM, I experienced many miraculous miracles. I witnessed people getting up out of wheel chairs and walking, blind eyes opened, and many more divine healings.

Just think, none of this would have happened if it hadn't been for God's messengers, those people from the church that wouldn't leave me alone.

Sam

[EDITORS' Note: Sam and Patty are involved in many Christian organizations and missions that are reaching the world for Jesus.]

Miracle 11

Trey
Forgiveness

But if ye forgive not men their trespasses, neither will your Father forgive your trespasses. (Matthew 6:15)

I had the knife in my hand and was about to cut the throat of the man I hated. I was a waiter in a nice restaurant and this same man, as luck would have it, was seated at my table. I had every reason to hate him because he had testified against me in court. I was convicted and sent to prison because of his witness against me. I thought to myself, "This man will not walk out of this restaurant alive today." Then a sermon, that I had heard preached while I was in prison, rang loud and clear in my soul. Remembering it kept me from committing murder.

A little black preacher, only about five-feet-two inches tall, with all his front teeth missing from street fighting, came and preached to us convicts. He preached on forgiveness a few months before I was released from jail. He was a very fiery little preacher, and what he said stuck in my soul forever. He was on the catwalk ministering to all that would listen. Then he spotted me. He came over to me and said, "Brother, you have a lot of unforgiveness in your life, but God can take all that hate away if you ask Him."

How did the little preacher know? How did he know that I had planned to kill the man who set me up in a drug deal? In fact, I was going to have this snitch killed while I was in prison. I had friends on the outside that would do the killing job for me. I would have a perfect alibi since I was in jail, and they would not be able to pin the crime on me. I had not only planned to kill this man, but I wanted him tortured for hours before he died as well. I wanted him to know that he was paying for squealing on me in court.

This little preacher read my mail that day. I never will forget what he quoted from the Bible, "For if you forgive men when they sin against you, your heavenly Father will also forgive you. But if you do not forgive men their sins, your Father will not forgive your sins" (Matthew 6:14-15 NIV). This Sermon on the Mount really got my attention. I chose to forgive the man I hated so much that day, but later on, when I got out of jail, I again had a real desire to kill him. And now I had him where I wanted him. He was at my table and I had the knife to end his life. Thank God the Holy Spirit intervened and overrode the will of the devil that was trying to make me commit murder.

When I was a child my Grandmother and I spent a lot of time together. We called Grandma, "Almo". At age seven I said, "Almo won't it be great to go to heaven one day?" "It'll be great, but you can't go unless you're saved," she said. I didn't know what "saved" meant so I said, "Are you saved Almo?" She said, "Yes I am!" And I asked, "Am I saved also?" She said, "No you're not and you're going straight to hell!" That statement really got my attention, and I planned one day to make sure that I was, in fact, saved. That day was a long time coming.

In my teenage years, I got into all the wrong things, with the wrong people, at the wrong places, and it almost cost me my life. I was just trying to fill the void in my heart with sex, drinking, drugs, and money. I was really in the fast lane trying to find what I was looking for in all the wrong places. I would even argue with folks who tried to get me straight and tell them I was doing okay, but on the inside I knew I was wrong. God began to put some speed bumps in my life, like being arrested several times and spending time in jail.

My mother was saved during my young years and prayed for me daily. God heard her prayers and spared me from the hell grandma told me about. I had been living my life for the devil but Mom's prayers were stronger than I was. I was heavy into the drug scene doing anything that would make me feel good for a while. I was a slow learner, but Mom continued praying for me, and the demons didn't stand a chance.

I was home one night watching a preacher on television talking about Jesus coming back. I went to my room and prayed to God. I said, "God, I have no desire to live for You, no desire to read Your Word, no desire to follow Your ways, and no desire to hang out with Your people." But I continued to say, "God please give me a desire for You and I will serve You all the days of my life."

While I was on my knees, God spoke to me and said, "I want your will!" Unfortunately, I did not surrender to God that night. Finally, about a year later, after the Lord and I had the same conversation four times, I said, "God, I surrender my will to You." I then went out partying with some friends and forgot about God again. But forty-eight hours later, God began to deal with me again big time! This just happened to be one year after I had been paroled from prison.

I went to my best friend's home after partying most of the night, and the devil attacked me there from 3:00 AM to 8:00 AM. Then I really called on God in desperation and He filled me with His Holy Spirit that very morning.

I'm a new man now, "born-again," and all old desires are gone. I now minister in prisons and try to tell the inmates about forgiveness and the love of Jesus like the little black preacher told me years before. I was teaching a group of men in jail a while back, and there was a big black man who seemed to be taking in all I was saying. He got up suddenly and grabbed one of the other inmates and said, "Brother, I forgive you and I love you." The other brother was really touched. Many inmates repented and asked others to forgive them that day.

I am so thankful that the Lord has saved me. He heard and answered by mother's prayers. Now it is my desire to deliver this soul-saving message to others before it is too late.

Trey

Miracle 12

Ron Knott
Helping the Poor

Blessed is he that considers the poor; the LORD will deliver him in time of trouble. (Psalm 41:1-2 NKJV)

God has intervened in my life many times since I started on the adventure of faith giving. "Here is the rest of the story," as Paul Harvey says. Because of the increase of my financial position I was offered many business deals. Most of them were not worthy of consideration. However, one friend asked me to invest in a shopping mall with him. He said, "This is a deal that won't fail. It will make us a lot of money." The fact is, the banker who was going to finance the project said, "Ron, if I were not restricted by bank regulations, I would go into partnership with you on this mall." I told these two gentlemen that I needed to leave the office for a few moments and consider the offer. I wanted to pray about it, and I did.

I am skeptical of many who say, "God told me this, or that." But, that day I believe that I heard God say loud and clear, "No! Do not invest in this mall." So I told my associates that I did not want in on the deal. Then they promised me everything! They increased the percentage of my ownership and said that I would never have to pay one penny. They said that they just needed my financial statement to help secure the loan. Then they really put me on a guilt trip by saying, "If you do not get in the deal we will loose $250,000 earnest money." You guessed it. I gave in. I signed the note for $1.5 million dollars. Why not? They assured me, "You can't lose on a deal like this, we will make a ton of money."

We bought the property for $4.7 million. It appraised for $12 million. Our company borrowed an additional $1.5 million to remodel the mall early in the venture. The $1.5 million note had to be guaranteed by each partner and I signed that contract. We expected to make about $7 million profit on this deal in a short time. Can't lose on a deal like that, so I thought. I was sure that I had mistaken the voice of God when the "NO" came during my prayer. I thought, surely this was the devil trying to keep me out of this lucrative deal.

The oil and gas industry took a nose dive shortly after we purchased the shopping mall and West Texas property lost value rapidly. This was during the time when asbestos in buildings was making headlines. Federal law required that this material be removed from all property and our mall was fabricated with tons of asbestos. Needless to say we could not sell the property, and the bank foreclosed. The $1.5 million was due and payable by all partners. One of my partners went back to Europe and the other one had no means to pay. I was the local target for collection. I was guilty. I had signed the note and I was responsible for the entire amount. Interest on this note exceeded $200,000 annually. My wife and I prayed profusely about this predicament. Now I was ready to listen and obey the Lord. This was my "belly of the whale" experience!

One morning, while praying, I flipped open my Bible roulette style. The pages opened to Psalms. The first thing I saw was Psalm 41:1-2 (NKJV) "Blessed is he who considers the poor; the LORD will deliver him in time of trouble. The LORD will preserve him and keep him alive; and he will be blessed on the earth; You will not deliver him to the will of his enemies." I do not remember ever having read that passage before. The words jumped off the page and into my troubled soul. I showed this revelation to my pastor and said, "God is going to make a way for me to pay that $1.5 million note."

I read and re-read that Scripture. Could God be telling me that He was able to deliver me out of this trouble? Then, like a message from heaven, I suddenly remembered the pledge that I had made and paid, to help the poor many months before. Part of that money went to pay doctor bills for those who could not pay. Part went to clothe the needy in Africa. Part went to support missionaries. God had not forgotten about my kindness to others. God had not forgotten His guarantees…His Word!

Within a few days after I read Psalm 41:1-2, I received a letter from the bank that stated, "The bank has canceled your $1.5 million note. You do not owe this bank one cent!" The other individuals were not released from the debt. Did I deserve that financial blessing? No! It was a gift from a loving God.

I only obeyed His Word concerning giving to the poor; His Word protected my welfare.

The greatest financial insurance available is to go into partnership with God. He is the greatest business partner one could hope to have. He has a lot of opportunities in which to invest. Lost souls, feeding and clothing the needy, supporting missionaries and faith giving are just a few guaranteed investments that one can add to his or her portfolio. My faith is not in the FDIC or FSLIC, but in FIJC (Faith In Jesus Christ).

Let me show you the kind of insurance I am talking about. The Lord impressed me to give $30,000 on a special project to help the needy. This was completely out of character for me, but my wife and I felt very strongly about making the pledge. This was many months before we purchased the mall that foreclosed. In fact, I had forgotten about giving the money when my financial crisis arose, but God had not forgotten. No one told me, or asked me to give to this need; I just felt a strong impression to give, so I made the pledge. This pledge was to be paid over a period of one year. Those were my terms with the Lord, because I did not have the money at the time of the pledge. This is called faith giving. If I have the money in my pocket then it takes no faith to give it. But, when I do not have the money and I am impressed to pledge by faith, the Lord honors that commitment by providing the funds for the pledge.

Soon after my pledge, the stock market hit an all-time low. My stocks and bonds lost more than the amount that I had pledged. I told my wife that we were going to pay the pledge even if we had to sell our home to do so! Within a short time God made a way for us to pay the pledge without selling anything. When my financial emergency arose, the Bank of Heaven and my advocate, Jesus Christ, responded quickly and resolved the problem in a way that I had never dreamed possible. Isn't that just like the Lord?

Ron

Miracle 13

Bill

Attacked by Demons

And saith unto him, All these things will I give thee, if thou wilt fall down and worship me. (Matthew 4:9)

Demons attacked me in my bedroom when I was twenty years old. This genuine assault frightened me beyond belief. I was in my bedroom asleep and alone, so I thought, when all of a sudden, I woke up with cold sweat all over my body. I could feel the presence of something in the room. I knew that I was not alone, that something was in there with me. I had chill bumps all over my body. I looked down at the foot of my bed and about a dozen little demons were trying to torment me. I could sense that their mission was to drag me to hell. I was not ready for such an invasion of my life and didn't know what to do about it. I finally called out to Jesus and they departed.

I had heard as a young kid, that Jesus had special power and could overcome anything. I sure needed His power that night and it worked. I knew I had to do something to keep these evil spirits away. They were frightful and a nuisance, to say the least. And I sure didn't want them coming back in my house.

A pastor lived next door to me and I knocked on his door early the next morning for help. I had stayed clear of the pastor in the past because I was afraid he would invite me to his church. I really didn't have time for church since my life was going very well doing it my way. I did what I wanted to do, when I wanted to do it. However, when the demons paid me a visit, I felt like the reverend and I should get better acquainted.

This godly preacher was very gracious to me the next morning. I was shocked, since I had thrown beer cans all over his property in the past. He explained how I could rid my house and my soul of demons forever. He prayed with me, and baptized me in the Name of the Lord. I never felt more secure and I knew that the demons could not penetrate the shield that was now wrapped around me.

This was the beginning of a great relationship with the pastor and his church family. In fact, I attended his church for over twenty years and grew in the Lord and His Word.

While attending the pastor's church I started a new company that built motorcycles. This company was manufacturing special sport motorcycles. They are, without a doubt, the best built bike that money can buy. I built the business from nothing to millions in sales in just a short time. The company was doing great.

However, I just got tired of running this business and sold it. I had gone through several tragedies that year and did not rely on God to help me through these times of unrest. My father died of cancer, my grandfather and grandmother died. I thought that God had deserted me, when in fact, I had deserted God. My successful business, that God had given me, consumed all my time. Pride and I placed God on standby in my life. I am thankful that He did not forget about me during that period.

My wife and I loved to ride motorcycles. We rode to every national park in the country. We rode through Yosemite National Park, Rocky Mountain National Forest, and Redwood National Forest just to name a few. We saw the beautiful landscapes that God had created. I knew that I needed to get back in relationship with God, but that could wait for a while, so I thought.

We were on our way back home after an excursion through the northwest. On the last day we were cruising through the beautiful mountains. It was such a beautiful day and the scenery was awesome. But all the fun changed to tragedy in one second.

As we rounded a curve, on a majestic mountaintop, we met a car head on in our lane. I didn't have time enough to take any evasive action and the car hit us head on. We were both thrown a great distance from the bike. I don't remember feeling any pain and didn't know if I was dead or alive. When I finally came to my senses, I started looking for my wife. Thank goodness she was just bruised up a bit. But I had a compound fracture in my leg and a cracked hip.

I was transported to a hospital and was unconscious for several weeks. After many operations, the doctors told me that it was essential that they take off my foot. My mom and wife said, "There is no way we'll let that happen because he will never be able to walk again." The doctors assured them that I would be able to walk as well with an artificial limb as I could before the accident. The foot came off and I have never been able to walk like I did before, no matter what the doctors said.

Finally, I was moved to a hospital in Texas. After one of my many examinations, I was returned to my room. As I was placed in the bed a man came into the room and asked for me. He then said, "I would like to speak with you for just a moment." I said, "Go ahead, I have all the time in the world." He said, "I'm from a little town several hundred miles away. God has sent me to give you a message. And I said, "Well, I hope it's a good one, since you've come such a long way and had a long wait while I was in the examination room."

He said, "God told me to tell you that He has been with you through everything that has happened to you. God has had his hand on you. You never blamed Him for what happened. You have gone through the trials of Job and He wants you to know that everything you do in the future will be blessed, as long you claim it in the Name of Jesus. You'll be blessed among all men the rest of your life as long as you put Him first in your life." And I said, "Wow." I knew that this message was from God.

I was eager to learn more from him and about him; however, I never saw him again. The man departed from my room and we could not locate him. I don't know his name, or where he came from. I do know that God sends angels. Regardless of whether he was an angel or not, the message that he delivered was the message that I needed to hear. From that day forward, my situation began to improve. The good days outweighed the bad days by far.

I started another high performance motorcycle and hot-rod company. But now I am using my company as a witnessing tool for Jesus. When I had the other company, I didn't have time to talk to anybody about Jesus and I really didn't want to. Now I've got so much to tell them. I've got so much to share. And when I talk to people about what God's done for me, I am utterly amazed at their interest and response I learned a long time ago that only what we do for God will last. All the rest will rust and decay, but what we do for the Lord will last forever.

Miracle 14

Ricky Sinclair
Escaped Prisoner

How shall we escape, if we neglect so great salvation? (Hebrews 2:3)

"Officer, can I use the restroom? I want to wash my hands." He said, "Yeah, but make it quick." With that few seconds of freedom, I ran past the jailer as fast as I could, through the front door, and out in the yard to freedom. The officer shouted, "Hey, hey, hey! Where are you going?" The deputy gave chase but I was just a little faster. I hit the chain link fence in the back yard of the jail, and with one leap vaulted over that structure.

This breakout kept me on the run for 56 days. All I had when I departed the jail was a pair of flip-flops for shoes, a thin tee shirt, and blue jeans. I ran into the woods barefooted. My feet were bleeding because of the many stickers I had picked up. My adrenaline was pumping loud and clear. But I could not stop because the law was hot on my heels. I knew that they would get the bloodhounds after me, so I ran figure eight patterns to confuse the dogs. By now my arms, face, and feet were bleeding from the briars in the thick brush of the Louisiana swamps. I heard helicopters coming my way. I went deeper into the swamp for cover. I could hear the four-wheelers coming my way. I saw about fifteen prison guards searching for me. I was experiencing anxiety and agony.

The search party seemed to be getting closer and closer. I had to dig in. I buried myself in a pile of leaves. Fire ants began eating the blood off my wounds. They continued on my face, neck, arms, and feet. They were between my toes, stinging like fire. I couldn't move or swat them because the guards were so close. The mosquitoes were also enjoying sucking my blood. I laid there for four nights and three days in complete misery! I began to hallucinate from dehydration.

One guard came within four feet of me. I could actually hear him breathing. But I still refused to give up. They had night sight goggles so the darkness did not help hide me. Bloodhounds walked all around me but they never picked up my scent. After the fourth day, they called off the hunt for me. I was then able to move about and find some stagnant water to drink.

My body ached. I wanted to give up. I was hungry, dirty, and very tired. I was also very confused and terribly alone. I had not eaten in four days. I found a deserted deer stand and made it my home for the next 52 days. I searched during the day for food. Blackberries were beginning to ripen. I ate armadillos raw, because I couldn't build a fire to cook with. I found old milk cartons and put the blackberries in them for days. They fermented and I was successful in making blackberry wine. I got drunk on this home-brew almost every night. I was a living caveman for fifty-six days and nights.

I had to get out of the predicament. I started back to civilization very cautiously. Hiding as much as I could along the way. I came upon a worker at a big plantation who had a phone. I told him I had got lost in the woods on a hunting trip and needed to call my mother to come get me. He looked at me like I was something from outer space, but finally allowed me to call mom. I asked her if she would come pick me up. She said, "No!" I started walking again and came upon some small kids playing in their back yard. I told them that I was lost and needed a ride home. Finally, they took me to their mother and she drove me home.

The nightmare was over. It had been hell for the past fifty-six days. The lady dropped me off at my home, but it was locked. I crawled in a back window. I found food, fresh clothing, and money. I also found vodka and leftover marijuana from my high school days. I got high.

Mom came in. She said, "Who are you?" "Mom, it's me. Ricky!" I must have really looked very bad for my own mother not to recognize me. She was afraid of me. We talked about me going to an aunt's home in Seattle. She would take me to another town and put me on a bus after dark. That was my plan.

Mom's boyfriend walked in. George and I were not friends and he was plenty scared when he saw me. He said he needed to go buy some cigarettes. I said, "No one leaves this house until I'm out of town!" Finally, I gave in to George's request to leave for smokes. I should have known what he would do. I was just not thinking clearly.

George returned in about thirty minutes with a swat team. They surrounded the house within seconds with M16 rifles in hand. They yelled, "OK! We know you are in there! We have got you surrounded! Come out with your hands up!" I crawled up in the attic and hid in a dark corner. They crashed the front door and came busting in mom's home. They yelled again, "We know you are in here! We will find you!" They searched for about twenty minutes and finally found a way up to the attic. My luck had just run out. I was soon handcuffed and taken back to where I had escaped from fifty-six days earlier.

How had I allowed myself to get in this dilemma to start with? I was raised in an alcoholic family and watched my mom and dad drink a fifth of booze every day of my life. Of course I inherited their lifestyle and ended up getting into some serious trouble with the law. I was busted for selling cocaine, marijuana, diazepam, and many other drugs at an early age. I had three felony convictions, and was facing a life sentence, when I escaped. I had been in jail before and sure didn't want to go back for life.

I had a very strange childhood. At age seven I developed spinal meningitis. It went into remission and came back again when I was twelve. The doctors said the odds of that happening are like being struck by lighting twice. This terrible disease should have killed me, but somehow God spared me.

Dad played music as a hobby and would take the entire family to where he was playing. I began stealing beer out of other people's ice chests when I was nine. Drinking beer seemed to be the "grown-up" thing to do.

My family was well respected in our community. We were members of the local Catholic church. We were wealthy in that dad owned a successful meat packing company, had 1900 acres of rich farm land, and 600 head of cattle. But both of my parents were hooked on alcohol. They hated drugs and told me to stay far away from them. On a drunken binge Dad said that he was god. He also boasted that nobody could take him down because of his wealth. Six months later, he developed cancer. The doctors gave him less than a year to live.

In the later stages of his cancer, a friend suggested that he start smoking marijuana to relieve the pain. I was shocked when I found him with the weed and reminded him of what he had told me. He said, "It is not wrong." He gave me a joint to smoke. I was thirteen at the time.

The next year, at fourteen, I was getting into a lot of trouble. Dad's condition declined and the radiation treatments were really rough on him. His business declined as well. We were losing money. I continued to smoke pot and was soon a dealer.

During my senior year I got arrested. The judge allowed me to graduate and sent me to jail. While I was in prison dad died. They reduced my sentence to let me out for the funeral. After the funeral I got back into the drug business big time. And there were many more acts of bad behavior that I was involved in.

After my fifty-six days on the run, I was back in jail again. One of the jailers, Officer James, came in to see me. He was the jailer on duty when I escaped. He told me that he wanted to deliver to me something that my mother had dropped off. It was a Bible that my praying aunt had sent me. Officer James told me that I should read it. He said, "You need Jesus to resolve your problems!" He also said, "Ricky, every answer you're looking for in life is in this Book." At the time, I was facing a lifetime prison sentence.

I read that Bible through and through several times. Each time I learned more about the God I never knew as a kid. I told another sheriff that I was called to preach, and of course he laughed at my jailhouse religion.

I went to court and was sentenced to seven years of hard labor at the Louisiana State Penitentiary in Angola, Louisiana. This is one of the toughest prisons in the USA. I still had other charges against me and could have spent the rest of my life behind bars.

I found out very quickly that homosexuality was alive in the prison system. It was sickening.

However, I was able to defend myself from such attacks. The first ninety days in prison were very rough. The guards would wake us up at 4:00 AM and put us in the fields digging with shovels. It was hard and hot. Many fights broke out and a lot of serious injuries occurred. Prison was no fun.

I got involved with the prison church that was run by the inmates. Everyone that attended was filled with the Holy Ghost. We would meet three nights a week for Bible study. A prison pastor, Bro. Robert Early, baptized me. He was a powerful man of God and had been in prison twelve years for bank robbery. He is now out and doing a great work for the Lord.

God spoke to me while I was in prison. He told me that I had a choice to make. If I chose sin, I would never see my family again. But, if I chose to serve Him, He would get me out of prison. I made a wise decision and chose to serve God. And true to His promise. He got me out of prison. I could have been sentenced to life but I was let out early.

As I walked out of prison my wife greeted me at the gate. After four years, I was free to go home. It was an answer to prayer. Jeannie, my wife, had fallen back, but very soon she asked for forgiveness and became on fire for God. I got a job repairing cars and Jeannie had a job as well. It was tough on our low pay but the Lord gave me a vision that I would soon be making more money. It happened as He said.

About five years ago my wife, our two boys and I started a church in our home. Soon we grew to twelve folks attending. In about six weeks, we had grown to sixty people. We had to look for a bigger place to meet. But we had no money. Finally, we were able to lease a conference room at a local hotel. In two years the congregation had grown to 250 members. Again, we started looking for a larger meeting place.

I found a nice building (shopping mall) that would suit our church needs, but the price was $1 million. We had less than $3,000 in the bank at that time. But, by faith I signed a purchasing agreement with a $2,000 check for the earnest money. Anybody knows that $2,000 will not buy a $1,000,000 building. But in addition to the $2,000 we had a lot of faith. His new church is called "The Miracle Place."

Within two weeks after I signed the purchase agreement, a loan institution said they had faith in our project and loaned us the money needed to close the deal.

We now have over 1000 members attending services in that shopping mall. We have eight full-time pastors, four secretaries, and all kinds of department heads. We started a program for those who were hooked on drugs and alcohol called the "All The Way House."

Many people are coming off the streets and go to a halfway house for treatment. But our house is an all-the-way-house. We found that all-the-way is how one gets free, not just halfway. When a person is willing to go all-the-way he can be set free. That is what it took for me and it is working for others as well. I tell folks that they must stay the course. Sin will always take you further than you want to go, keep you longer than you planned to stay, and cost you more than you planned to pay. Our motto is, "Win the lost at any cost, because people last for ever." It costs us our time, our money, our privacy, and everything else, but it is worth it.

Ricky

[EDITORS' Note: Ricky now has three large churches, that have over 1000 members each, and he is building more. God used his availability, and gave him the ability to do the impossible in winning the lost. Read Ricky's book "Miracle at Large" for more details about his life and ministry.]

Miracle 15

Ann

Pledged One Million Dollars

Every man according as he purposeth in his heart, so let him give; not grudgingly, or of necessity: for God loveth a cheerful giver.
(2 Corinthians 9:7)

My husband turned to me and said, "We are going to pledge one million dollars to Campus Crusade for Christ." I said, "We are going to do what?" Again he said, "I am pledging $1 million to Campus Crusade for Christ, tonight." And I said, "Have you lost your ever-loving mind? You know that we can just barely pay our bills with our income now. No, on second thought we are in debt now, we can't possibly pay all our bills. So how in God's name do you expect us to give this organization a million dollars?" He said, "I don't know how we will get the funds, all I know is the Lord told me, tonight, to make the million dollar pledge, and I did. It is not in our hands now. The Lord will provide."

I went to bed angry that night because of the ludicrous statement that my husband had made. My husband was just not thinking. I had filed for bankruptcy protection early on in our marriage and sure didn't want to get in that financial predicament again.

We were at a Campus Crusade for Christ meeting that night and Dr. Bill Bright gave all of the attendees a challenge to pledge a million bucks for the work of the Lord. That fabulous organization spreads the Gospel worldwide and surely deserves all the money it can raise. The only problem is we didn't have the money to give, so I thought.

When I awoke the next morning God told me, "Sign the pledge card and I will provide the million dollars." I had to apologize to my husband that morning and let him know that the Lord had also told me the same thing. Doug and I signed the pledge card. And would you believe in just a few short years we were able to give $1 million to Campus Crusade for Christ? That was a faith pledge in action. God had said that if we would make the pledge He would provide the funds. We did and He did!

This allowed us to partner with Campus Crusade in their seventy ministries worldwide. The "Jesus Film" is sponsored by that organization and has led thousands to Christ. We were blessed by just being a small part of the mission.

Years earlier I was led into witchcraft by a group of so-called Christians. They had a class in a well-known church called "Inter Strength Through Personal Faith." The name sounds innocent enough, but they believed in and practiced fortune telling, tarot cards, horoscopes, and other witchcraft rituals. And they actually believed that this medium, for future information, was not against Christian teachings. I learned later that the Lord hates such clairvoyant activities.

There was an older man, Stan Kirkland, in the class who challenged their teachings with the Bible. Of course he was not very popular and was told basically to keep his mouth shut. In fact he really irritated me, especially when he would say, "But the Bible says…." In fact I turned to him in one class and told him, "Shut-up! I don't care what the Bible says." The old devil can blind your mind when you are not "born-again."

This kind old gentlemen kept his cool and said, "Young lady if you will allow me to come to your home I will answer the questions about witchcraft that you don't even know how to ask." I was so arrogant and full of myself at that time in my life that I said; "Just come," and gave him my address.

He and a Christian lady appeared the next Monday morning at my front door ready to share the Gospel with me. They were part of a group called "Evangelism Explosion," which I had never heard of. In the past I had thrown people out of my dorm room, who were loaded with tracts and trying to convert me to whatever they believed. "Today was not going to be any different," so I thought. I would get rid of these proselytes very quickly. But when this lady said, "Jesus is God, and He came in the flesh and died for me," something like a bolt of lighting struck my heart. My soul was hungry for what this lady was telling me and I knew it was TRUTH, but I still was not quite ready for the big change.

The lady left me a copy of the "Gospel of John." I read it from cover to cover many times. It had a little prayer in the back for accepting Jesus and I prayed it every day until they came back the next Monday. When they came in I was ready for all the Lord had for me. I even joined their church and became a teacher in the "Evangelism Explosion" class.

I wish I could say I lived happily ever after, but that was not the case. I grew cold in the Lord and just put Him on the shelf for a while. I even took my kids out of the Christian school. However, God did not forget about me. I was so miserable without Him.

Finally, I begged Him to take me back. And He did.

Later on we got involved in missions and actually went to Kenya and Nairobi, Africa. I fell in love with Africa and that is where my heart is today. The people have so many needs. We Americans are so blessed and the Africans are so poor as a whole.

We met a young man on our trip. His name is George. It was very unique how George came into our life. First, my daughter met

George. She was very excited and told us that we needed to meet the young man and give him some financial aid. She did not tell us his name at that time. Of course we told her that there were many in Africa that needed help and that we appreciated the fact that she demonstrated a charitable heart, but it was impossible to solve every need.

The next day I met a young man and felt a lot of love and compassion for him. I told my husband that I had met a young man that we needed to help. My husband repeated the words we had for our daughter the day before about not being able to help everyone. So I just kind of forgot about this young fellow.

My husband went jogging the next day and while exercising he met a young man that he really liked. He was quick to say, "We need to help this young man." Of course my daughter and I gave him the same lecture that he had given us when we wanted to help two other young men. Finally, we compared notes and discovered that the three young men that we had met individually were actually the same young man, George. Was this a coincidence, or was it the hand of God?

We all loved George so we elected to help bring him to the United States to finish his schooling. We felt like this would be compassion in action on our part. George came to America, with our help, and is about to graduate from a large Bible school. We are so proud of him.

It has been a thrill letting God direct our life. We have learned to trust Him for every need. I pray that you will do the same.

Ann

Julianna
Atheist Turned Evangelist

Stand therefore, having your loins girt about with truth, and having on the breastplate of righteousness. (Ephesians 6:14)

"You are not my child; I am not your mother; I am only your grandmother. Your mama left you when you were three months old and I have raised you." I can still hear the emptiness and hurt that statement caused me that day. I was only five years old, but I allowed grief to make my life a living hell for years.

Grandma must have been upset with me that day to deliver such a stunning blow to my little heart. She is a wonderful lady, and I thought she was my mother until that very dreadful day. But, I learned that day that my mother never wanted me nor did my dad. I spent the majority of my life wondering why they didn't love me? That question devastated me. The knowledge of that rejection caused me a lot of hurt, anger, and a life of rebellion. "There must be something wrong with me," were my thoughts. Mama never came back or made any contact with me. That hurt me more than her leaving. She could have at least sent me a birthday card, but I never received anything from her when I needed it most.

My only friend, so I thought, was my uncle. He got me hooked on marijuana, alcohol, and showed me how to stick a needle in my arm when I was eleven. Later he showed me a lot of pornography and began molesting me.

I quit school in the eighth grade because I was hooked on marijuana. I married at fifteen and had my first child, Amber, when I was sixteen.

I started drinking, and later on became a topless dancer in nightclubs. I even joined a Buddhist group. Then I claimed to be an atheist. I was so mixed up. I met my first husband when I was fifteen and he told me very quickly that there was a God and we were going to serve Him. We started going to church. I got clean from drugs and the other filth for a while. However, that didn't last long and I was soon back in my old habits again.

I divorced my first husband and married a dope dealer. That marriage lasted ten years, but it was ten years of pure hell. We had a son, Gabriel, during that marriage. I needed to make more money to help pay for my kids' care. I enrolled in a medical assistance class and graduated with honors, but I couldn't find a job. Finally, I started topless dancing again because the pay was very good. This only got me hooked on more drugs. It seemed like everything I tried ended up getting me in more trouble.

After about one year of topless dancing, I got into real trouble with the law. I had left my kids in the car, alone, for about fifteen minutes. The kids were not hurt, thank God, but the DA placed me on probation. I discovered cocaine while I was on probation and got hooked on that drug.

They locked me up and I was a basket case for about one month. I was miserable in jail. I said to the Lord, "Please open these doors and let me go to hell." Thank goodness He didn't obey my request.

He knew that I didn't want to go to hell and in my own way I was asking for help. I really wanted to be with my children and I wanted and needed someone or something to love me. I didn't want my kids feeling rejected by their mother, as I had felt rejected by mine. I knew I had to get out of jail and back to them.

Finally, I cried out to God. I said, "God, I'm so sorry, please forgive me." At that moment of forgiveness I felt the love of Christ come all over me. It was a most wonderful and warm feeling. I felt love for the first time since I was five years old. I told God that I would do whatever He wanted me to do. I started reading a Bible, signed up in the Chaplain's program, and attended every Christian program that was offered in jail.

When I got out of jail I really started serving the Lord. My husband, Greg, and I are going to Bible school. We get up every morning and quote the armor of God Scriptures in Ephesians 6:14, "Stand therefore, having your loins girt about with truth, and having on the breastplate of righteousness"; and Isaiah 54:17, "No weapon that is formed against thee shall prosper; and every tongue that shall rise against thee in judgment thou shalt condemn. This is the heritage of the servants of the LORD, and their righteousness is of me, saith the LORD."

We are totally free from all past desires when we read those Scriptures every morning. We walk in freedom everyday. And it is my desire that the readers of this testimony will allow God to bestow love on them each day, when others may not show any love or affection. I found my true family and friend in the person of Jesus Christ.

More good news is the fact that my mother and I are now good friends. We talk at least once a week.

That was another real healing miracle of forgiveness. God is good.

Julianna

Miracle 17

Billie
Topless Dancer

…for I will forgive their iniquity, and I will remember their sin no more.
(Jeremiah 31:34)

I had to get some drinks in me before I could go out and dance "topless" before these men who gawked at my body. You would think that after four years in this profession, I would have become "shameless" doing my routine night after night. But something held me back. I had to erase the guilt feelings with booze before performing each night. Tequila seemed to take my humiliation away and give me more freedom on stage. The more tricks, and the more movements I would perform was directly related to the tips received. As a matter of fact, once the dance started, and the men commenced yelling and reacting like a group of hungry lions then I felt very good about my body and myself. This feeling of accomplishment soon replaced my shame with pride.

My profane way of life started when I was very young. My mother spent a lot of time in bars and I was always with her. My parents had divorced when I was one year old. I saw many fights and other lewd things going on during my early childhood. I thought I could handle anything the world had to offer.

At age fourteen, I told my mother I was leaving home. She really didn't care, in fact, she was probably glad that I was getting out of her way. I hit the streets, slept on park benches, stayed with anybody who would invite me, got hooked on dope, and was raped twice.

A friend about my same age and I would sleep in cars that we could break into. Then we started stealing cars and would sell them to have money for a motel room. Stealing cars gave us a rush. Like taking dope, it was our way of having fun. We started breaking into apartments and homes to steal money for food. We were always in trouble. It is obvious that God had His hand on me during this time in my life or I would have been dead long ago.

I met a man and his wife while on the beach in Galveston. After hearing my story they invited me to come live with them. The lady seemed very nice and I was excited about finally having a place to stay. She said, "You can come and stay with me and my husband, and watch our kids." But, this turned out to be a real weird situation. Their purpose was for me to help them heighten their sexual activities. They were perverted and demonic, to say the least. The man would come in my bedroom and take his liberty with me while the lady watched.

I got pregnant when I was eighteen while I was still on the streets. I didn't know what I was going to do, or where I was going to go.

I didn't have a way to provide for my child. I asked my friends for advice and they suggested I start working at a strip club. I started out as a waitress, but the owner wanted me to dance "topless." I cried the first two nights that I performed; thereafter, all it took was a couple of drinks.

This sort of activity started a huge downward spiral in my life. I guess you can say that I went from bad to worse. I experienced the worst in people. This brought a sense of hopelessness in my mind. I thought that there were no good people in the world, and that I had no good future. All the people I knew were perverted. I hated people and I hated life.

I had gone to church a few times as a kid. They had free food so my mother would send us there just to eat. I don't remember much about the service.

After having my son, I began to see things much differently. Soon after his birth I read a book that changed my life. The name of the book was "A Divine Revelation of Hell," by Mary K. Baxter.

In Mary Baxter's book she described how Jesus took her to hell to see how terrible it really is. The pits of hell were full of fire and people were screaming to get out. Their flesh was on fire, and worms were crawling over their bodies, but the flesh was not consumed like it says in the Bible. She described seeing a woman in hell whose skeleton body was burning. Her eye sockets were on fire, but she could see Jesus and cried out for mercy. Jesus had sadness in his face, and He told her that judgment was set and He could not change her sentence. He told the woman, "I died for you, but you let the pleasures of your life override my many pleas for you to come to Me."

She wrote of seeing another woman who was a backslider, screaming in agony for Jesus to forgive her. Mary related that it looked like the woman was about to get out of this fiery pit, but a demon came and knocked her back into the flames. She said that Jesus wants us to know that we serve a God of love and a God of judgment as well.

I had nightmares after reading this book. I suggest you buy the book for all friends and family. It changed my life. In fact you can hear the entire story on the Internet and download it free at www. spiritlessons.com.

I read the book many times. It was so real. It let me know that I sure do not want to spend eternity burning like these poor souls.

I decided, after reading this book, that I must go to church. When I finally went, I was very surprised to find some of my kinfolk there. I found out that my second cousin and her husband were the pastors. Also, my aunt was attending. The Lord knew exactly what I needed. I had never had a family before.

God began to pull back the layers from my heart. I started telling the people at my club that they were going to hell. Of course they didn't want to hear that! Eventually I quit going to the club. I just threw up my hands and surrendered to Jesus.

Now I have a future for my son and we are living in victory. I have a wonderful place to live, thanks to the fine folks of my church. A lady at the church had a garage apartment that needed a little fixing, and she agreed to let me stay there.

Before I moved in I went by the apartment one evening and was surprised to find many of the church members there painting, cleaning and putting furniture in place. They even put in kitchenware, pillows, and a TV. Of course I just bawled like a baby. No one had ever done anything like that for me before.

I've told people time after time that fear drove me to the church because I didn't want to go to hell, but the love of the people and the example of Christ they set for me is what truly changed my life.

After becoming a Christian, I finished my high school degree and also graduated with my two-year college degree. I'm now a teacher at the church and my son is enrolled there. God put me right where I needed to be.

I should have been dead long ago, due to my lifestyle. My heavenly Father protected me and brought me to the knowledge of His son Jesus Christ and Himself. I can never thank Him enough. May God bless you and yours.

Billie

Miracle 18

Larry Flenniken
Intercessory Prayer

*So shall my word be that goeth forth out of my mouth: it shall not
return unto me void, but it shall accomplish that which I please, and it
shall prosper in the thing whereto I sent it. (Isaiah 55:11)*

Blood was gushing from the large wound in my back. The enemy
had made an accurate shot and brought me down on the battlefield.
The medic said, "Larry, every time your heart beats, blood squirts
about two feet high." I could feel myself getting weaker and weaker
with every heartbeat. "Am I going to make it doc?" His honest reply
was, "I don't know."

The helicopter had just dropped a group of us army infantrymen
off in a hot battle zone in the Republic of Vietnam. I was in an
artillery unit but was assigned to this infantry squad. Our squad had
only been on the ground for about forty-five seconds when I took a
round in my back. The blast knocked me about fifteen feet. I knew I
was injured very badly, but I just didn't know how serious.

Spiritually, I was not ready to die. I had been raised a Christian
but in my teenage years I got away from that teaching and was
doing my own thing. Many of my friends had been drafted and sent
to Vietnam. Then I also got my greeting card from Uncle Sam and I

was soon headed for Vietnam with the U.S. Army. The army treated me well and I was honored to be selected "Soldier of the Year" by my peers. However, this honor didn't keep me off the front lines of battle.

As I lay there bleeding, I prayed and asked God to let me live. I also asked the Lord to have others pray for me as well. I recall, as a kid, that intercessory prayer would get results from the Lord. I was very fearful and needed a quick miracle, or I would die in that faraway country.

The area we were fighting in was so hostile that helicopters assigned to medical evacuation units were told not to enter our region. In fact the army had lost fifty-seven helicopters and crews in the past few days on such rescues. Therefore, my chances of getting flown out of that fearful area to a field hospital were slim to none. In fact, I did not want another chopper crew shot up, just to rescue me. The area was just too unsafe.

Little did I know that halfway around the world, the Lord placed my need on a group of Christians who were having a Tuesday night Bible study. In fact, my mother was in that group of believers in Flint, Michigan. She interrupted the Bible study by saying, "Something is very wrong with my son Larry. We need to pray for him now!" Of course the little group entered into intercessory pray for me and prayed most of the night. They didn't have a clue that I had been wounded and that I was in very grave condition. The Holy Ghost placed me on their hearts and let them know that I needed prayer. I am so glad that He did.

Their prayers were amplified in heaven that night, and God responded. One of my favorite sayings now is, "Prayer commands heaven."

There was a chopper flying high overhead our operating area. The pilot could see that there was a big firefight going on below him. He also overheard radio transmissions about a seriously wounded soldier that needed to be taken to the field hospital. The pilot was not part of the medical evacuation group. He was returning from another mission and just happened to be in our area. Something told him to drop in for the rescue. Our commanders said, "No, it is much too dangerous." He kept coming.

The door gunners of the chopper were very upset because their pilot had put them in harm's way to save me. They kept their machine guns blazing in all directions while the pilot hovered for the rescue. I was loaded on board quickly and we lifted off. The chopper was hit several times while climbing out. I thought I would be killed, for sure, before we got out of that area. But somehow, we made it to the field hospital. I was told later that the helicopter was damaged so much in the rescue attempt that it never flew again.

God had heard and answered the prayers of the little group in Flint, Michigan and my life was spared. This miracle in action let me know the power of prayer and the mercy of God. Soon I was out of the hospital and on my way home with my second Purple Heart.

After Vietnam, I came back home and rededicated my life to the Lord. I had several jobs, but seemed to be very unstable because of the trauma I experienced in the war. I worked for General Motors for a while, but I just was not happy there. I quit that job and started working at a health club. One day I saw a man pass the club that resembled one of my fellow soldiers in Vietnam. I said, "Jimmy is that you?" He wheeled around and recognized me on the spot.

My wife and I had Jimmy over to our home many times in the next few months. He knew almost nothing about God or the Bible. He was the kind of guy that went all-out for whatever he was doing. My wife invited him to our church. And Jimmy found God that night and got very excited. He said, "When I received the Holy Ghost, it was like the sun came down and kissed the earth and I was right in the middle of the smack."

Jimmy loved the Lord and became a mature Christian very quickly. God and the church became his life. He bought a beautiful new suit to wear to church. My way of bragging on the suit was to say jokingly, "Jimmy, when you die I want you to leave me that suit." He said, "Larry, that is a deal."

It was only a short time later that Jimmy said, "Larry it looks like you are going to get the suit soon." I said, "What do you mean?" He said, "I just came from the doctor and they tell me I have less than 90 days to live." I was crushed. It appears that he was a victim of Agent Orange that was used to defoliate the trees in Vietnam. Many servicemen and women died after leaving Vietnam, who were exposed to Agent Orange while serving in that country.

Jimmy's weight dropped from 170 pounds to 80 pounds in just a few weeks. He lost his hearing and became blind. But his love for the Lord grew even more. As I was walking down the hall of the hospital to visit Jimmy, I could hear him singing. He sang, "If God is dead who is this living in my soul?"

I suppose my tear dropped on his arm as I leaned over his bed. He said, "Larry, is that you? Don't cry. I had a dream last night and the Lord said that He is taking me home today." About eight hours later Jimmy departed this world to live with his Savior.

Several years later when I was preaching a revival in Chicago, I noticed a fellow in the back of the church who seemed to be very excited about something. He came up to the front of the church and said, "I am the helicopter pilot who rescued you on February 4, 1967 in Vietnam." We both were completely amazed. I had not seen or heard from him since that dreadful day in Vietnam.

He had been shot down a couple of months after my rescue and was discharged from the army due to injuries he received during the crash. After leaving the army, he moved to Odessa, Texas and there turned his life over to the Lord. His company had transferred him to Chicago and he had just walked into this service as a visitor that night. We both were shocked and thrilled about how the Lord arranged our meeting. And he was especially overwhelmed that I was a preacher. By the way, my text that night was, "Not by chance, but by divine appointment."

I had the honor of being President of "Rolling Thunder." This is a group of 250,000 motorcyclists that ride from California to

Arlington, Virginia each Memorial Day to lay a wreath on the grave of the Unknown Soldier.

As you can tell by my testimony, the Lord has blessed my family and me. Prayer is the only reason that I am here.

I am now the pastor of a church in Sherman, Texas. God bless.

Larry Flenniken

Corina

Drugs and Stealing

Let him that stole steal no more: but rather let him labour, working with his hands the thing which is good…. (Ephesians 4:28)

"Dear Jesus, please make my daddy come home," I prayed. I was eleven years old when my parents separated. I was so afraid that daddy would never come back. I needed him so much.

My family did not go to church before daddy left. However, I knew that there was a little Pentecostal church nearby. The church had a bus that came through our neighborhood and picked up kids that wanted to go church. Mama let me go with them. I asked the pastor to pray that my daddy would come home. He said, "We will both pray. All you have to do is to believe that the Lord will bring your dad home and it will happen."

That night I heard my dad coming home in the early hours of the morning. I could hear him asking my mother if he could come back home, and she agreed. I was so happy. The Lord had answered my prayer that very day.

The entire family started going to church after dad came home. But, as I got older, I let other activities interfere with my church going. I quit going to the house of worship and this was not good.

I was a six-foot tall girl in the sixth grade, and this caused me to be very self-conscious of my physique. Most everyone at school made fun of me because of my height. They would call me "bean pole" and other derogatory names. This gave me a very bad inferior complex and caused me to have very little self-worth. As a result of their embarrassing attacks about my appearance, I started taking drugs just to overcome the ridicule I was facing from other students. Drugs led me to stealing and other shameful acts. I completely forgot about God during this period of my life and all that He had done for me and for my family.

A short time later my sister was in a terrible auto accident. The doctors told us that she was not going to live. They suggested to my parents that we should have the life-support equipment removed and let her die. My parents said, "No!" I cried out to the Lord for help. I pleaded with God to let my sister live, and I told Him I would start serving Him again. Miraculously, my sister started improving and was soon released from the hospital.

I started going back to church, but I only went for about three weeks. Soon I was back to my old ways again. I was ultimately arrested for doing dope and stealing. My parents did not have the money to bail me out of jail, so I served my entire sentence of seven months. I was nineteen years old at the time.

Serving time in jail was actually a blessing for me, although I hated being locked up. A wonderful Christian lady, who had a calling for prison ministry, would spend hours teaching me the Word of God. She was a great teacher and I learned a lot about Jesus from her. When I was released from jail, I started attending home Bible studies. I was very impressed with those who attended the studies. They appeared very holy, but most of them had a rap sheet longer than mine. I didn't understand how they had made the change from sinner to saint seem so easy.

God gave me a vision of me being led up a hill to be crucified for my sins. I knew that I was guilty, but I was too young to die. Again, I called out to God for help. As I was being led up the hill to be nailed on the cross, a man came along and pushed me back. He said, "I will die for your sins." Of course that Man was Jesus. This was His way of letting me know that He had already paid the price for my sins, and all I had to do was accept what He had done.

Up to that point in my life I knew Jesus as Savior, but I did not know Him as Lord. When I made Jesus "Lord" my lifestyle really changed.

After I confessed Jesus as Lord of my life, I was never the same. I passed out tracts and other literature at many events and got involved in many Christian activities. I am now married to a pastor, and we have seven children.

God changed my life, answered my prayers, and saved my soul. He is eagerly waiting to do the same for others. God bless.

Corina

Muhammad
What is God's Name?

Neither is there salvation in any other: for there is none other name
under heaven given among men, whereby we must be saved.
(Acts 4:12)

I come from a strong Muslim family. When we were young my father forced us to go to the mosque and obey all the rituals. Yet I wouldn't just pray because I had to; I would cry out with tears, "God, I want to know you. Talk to me."

I was on a train, and I saw a foreigner sitting quietly. I said, "Hello, my name is Muhammad." He smiled and said, "Hi, my name is Bill." We talked until we reached his destination. He gave me his address and said, "Come visit and we'll talk more."

My heart was restless; I couldn't forget about that man. The following week I visited him, and we soon became good friends.

One day I found him sitting in his living room with a dark face instead of his usual smile. He was reading the newspaper and he said, "Muhammad, I think we can never be friends." He showed me a newspaper article that said Muslims could never have friendships with Christians.

I replied, "Bill, you don't understand. We can be friends, but your faith is different." I had been thinking that I should share Islam with him and bring him to the mosque. Now was the moment! So I said, "Bill, what you believe is wrong."

He said, "Remember that today you have asked to talk about religion. I did not ask you." [Restrictions in Muhammad's country bar Christians from actively proselytizing]. I agreed. We went to his office and closed the door.

Bill showed me a Koran (Islam's holy book) in my language, not Arabic. "Being a Christian, I have a Koran," he said. "Being a Muslim, do you have a New Testament?" I said, "No, why should I? It is rejected." He asked, "Where does your Koran say that? Can you show me a single verse?" I responded, "Well, I have heard it from the imam [Muslim worship leader]."

I had never read the Koran in my own language. Bill showed me some verses where it said we should read the previous books, not just the New Testament but the books of Moses and the prophets. I was so surprised that I grabbed the book from his hands. Why had I never heard this before?

Then he asked, "Why do you think what I believe is wrong?" I said, "Bill, you believe in Jesus. We do too, but as a prophet, not as God. How can God have a son? You shouldn't say that; it is a grave sin. You will be burned in hell forever. Friend, I want to save you."

Bill said, "Open your eyes. Open your heart. God is not limited, my friend. He made you and will show himself to you. Ask him."

I went home with a storm in my heart. I was so accustomed to following a culture, a ritual. But I kept praying. Bill helped me know more from the Koran, from the Bible, and from different books as well. Then he gave me the names of some other Muslims who had accepted Christ. They said, "Brother, we were in darkness. Now we are God's children.

I couldn't eat; I couldn't sleep. Bill saw the restlessness in my heart and said, "Muhammad, I think you've read enough books. This is the time to challenge God. Find a quiet place, close the door and kneel before him. Ask him to come to you in the name of Buddha, in the Hindu gods' names, in Mohammed's name and in Jesus' name. See which name he answers."

Late one night I thought, "This is the time." I washed my face, came to my room and closed the door and windows. I knelt before God and put a chair in front of me, like he would come and sit there. I said, "God, all these years I have prayed to you. You know my heart. I want to know you. I need to challenge you. Talk to me. If you are the God who created me, I ask you to come to me in Buddha's name."

I waited. I got no answer. Then I said, "I ask you to come to me in the name of all those Hindu gods. If this is the way you want me to worship you, I will worship those idols." I waited five minutes, ten minutes and got no answer.

Then I started praying in the name of Muhammad. My heart was heavy, because I always had such respect toward Muhammad, the holy, beloved prophet of God. I told God, "All these years I have been praying to you through Muhammad. The time has come now to ask you if Muhammad is the anointed one." There were tears in my eyes. I waited, ten, twenty, thirty minutes and still no answer.

Then, unwillingly, I said, "If you want me to pray in Jesus' name, if he is your real anointed one, I ask you to come and talk to me."

Let me tell you, I didn't have to wait thirty minutes! Right at that moment, I felt like someone walked into my room. The hair on my body stood up. I felt from my feet to my head that somebody was touching me.

I heard a voice saying, "Muhammad, I am Jesus, your Lord. I love you. Do you want to know anything more?" I cried, "No, my Lord. I trust you! You are my Lord from today. All these years I have been worshiping god, and he never answered. Today, You answered."

I didn't sleep that night. Such joy filled my heart that I had never felt before.

The next day I went to see Bill. Before I said anything, he understood. He hugged me and said, "Son, are you ready?" I said, "Yes, I'm ready." In his living room I made my profession of faith. I wanted to be baptized, but he asked me to wait and learn more. Later that year I was baptized.

From that day on, God has had such mercy and grace for this sinner. To this day I am serving Jesus in His ministry.

Muhammad

Miracle 21

Cindy
Gay Lifestyle

...for even their women did change the natural use into that which is against nature. (Romans 1:26)

My sex change, that I had planned so carefully, was interrupted when my Grandmother found a letter from one of my female partners. In this letter it was very obvious that I was living a gay lifestyle since it was composed of very intimate details of my relationship with this gay partner. I thought that I hid my lifestyle very well, but the Lord allowed Grandma to find this tell-all letter.

"Your Grandfather would turn over in his grave if he knew you were mixed up in this sort of thing," Grandma said. I loved my Grandparents very much and did not want to hurt either of them. They had raised me from an early age since my parents divorced when I was very young. Grandpa had died a couple of years before and I really missed him. At that moment I said to myself, "I'll just put off the sex change until after Grandma passes away."

My Grandparents were members of a Pentecostal church and were devout Christians. We lived in a small community in Texas and attended church regularly. I later moved in with an aunt and out from under the scrutiny of my Grandmother. There I was able to do what I wanted to do.

At the age of eight a neighborhood girl introduced me to the homosexual lifestyle. After that one incident I was a changed person. Something happened to me and I began to think I was a man or should be changed into a man and that I should have sexual relationships with only women. Later I would learn this is a spirit that possesses homosexuals.

Gay people are not born, they are created by the works of Satan. The second lie that Satan is publishing across the nation is that 10% of the population is gay. The accurate number is less than 2% are gay. The devil increased the percentage to make people think it is a normal lifestyle. It is a fact that homosexuals have high death rates not only from AIDS but also from violence, substance abuse, cancer, suicide, and murder.

The gay lifestyle led me into all kinds of illegal drugs by the time I was thirteen. The drugs helped me overcome my attitude as a lesbian. I felt completely normal playing the role as a male in my relationships with others. I noted that most of the girls on the high school basketball team were lesbians as well. So I felt that I was doing the right thing.

After high school I went from one relationship to another. My life was a complete mess. Later on I went to work in Las Vegas. My life was more out of control. I was very depressed after breaking a relationship with my gay partner and felt like the whole world had turned on me. My sister knew of my problem and tried to help. In fact she came to Vegas and brought me back to Texas.

Grandmother had died and so had one of my brothers. My sister allowed me to live with her when I came back to Texas. They were church members but did not try to push their religion on me, but they did invite me to Sunday morning service and I went. I knew that I would not be swayed by their beliefs. Everyone knew that Christians hated gay people. Of course that is another lie of the devil. Christians hate sin, but love the sinner.

As I set my foot in the door of that church it was like a bolt of lighting hit me. I had not cried in years. But there was something that made my eyes run like rivers of water flowing down my cheeks. My sister noticed my condition and led me to the altar. Before I reached the altar I began to speak in tongues. The Lord baptized me with the Holy Spirit. I was really "born-again" as the girl He designed me to be in the first place.

I am sure that both my Grandparents were dancing in their graves when they saw my conversion. Their prayers for me had not returned void. I am thankful to God for His mercy and grace that spared me even though I was in that awful lifestyle for so long.

Jesus is willing and able to save homosexuals, alcoholics, drug addicts, mass-murderers, and all other sinners. We just need to share the TRUTH with them in a loving way before they step into eternity.

Cindy

[EDITORS' NOTE: The agenda of the gay community is to lie about this terrible addiction. The following facts are taken from Mission America.

It is an unfortunate fact that advocates of homosexuality, including teachers, students, administrators, teachers' union delegates, and school board members, are now permitted to promote homosexuality in a variety of ways in many school districts. Curricular materials and extra-curricular programs implying or proclaiming acceptance of homosexual behavior are becoming more and more common. These are frequently initiated through school alliances with influential homosexual pressure groups such as GLSEN (Gay, Lesbian and Straight Education Network) and PFLAG (Parents, Families and Friends of Lesbians and Gays). Local resistance is suppressed as advocates receive pro bono legal support from the ACLU, the Lambda Legal Defense Fund, the National Education Association's legal defense for homosexual teachers, and other groups.

Most of this is flying under the radar of parents and communities. Yet this betrayal of trust has become a public health and social stability issue for virtually every community, as the majority of students educated in public or secular schools, even if raised in Christian homes, are now being successfully indoctrinated with the belief that engaging in homosexual behavior is a right and is relatively harmless. The truth is otherwise. Homosexual behavior presents many serious risks, and those risks are well-documented.

With homosexual behavior comes a whole host of very significant health and lifestyle risks. Whether high-risk conduct is a result of homosexual desires, or contributes to developing them, or some of both, is anyone's guess. The fact remains that teens engaging in homosexual behavior are participating in a lifestyle that:

1. Reduces life expectancy at age twenty by at least eight to twenty years.

2. Increases, by at least 500%, the risk of contracting AIDS.

3. Increases the risk of contracting a sexually transmitted disease by nearly 900%.

4. Increases by 4,000% the risk of developing anal cancer.

5. Substantially increases the likelihood of smoking, having mental health disorders (other than same-sex attraction), being the victim of "domestic" violence, and being involved in alcohol and drug abuse.

6. Substantially increases the likelihood of contracting hepatitis and other gastrointestinal infections.

7. Substantially increases the risk of contracting bacterial vaginosis, breast cancer, and ovarian cancer.

8. Has high levels of participation in sadomasochism, coprophilia, fisting, and other dangerous, deviant sex practices

9. Involves extraordinarily high levels of promiscuity.

As it now stands, each child enrolled in a public school is likely to receive numerous direct and implicit messages at school that homosexual behavior should be accepted as normal. The underlying (and erroneous) assumptions of these messages are:

1. That homosexuality is inborn and inevitable for some students and teachers and therefore a matter of "rights." There is no body of scientific research that establishes this proposition.

2. That homosexual behaviors add no higher risk than current trends in heterosexual behavior. This is not supported by public health data or common sense.

3. That homosexuality is a viewpoint and should be protected by "free speech" constitutional protections. Like smoking, it is actually a high risk behavior. Schools should no more permit homosexual behavior to be presented to children as "normal" and "acceptable" than smoking or drug use should be presented to children as "normal" and "acceptable".

4. That objections to homosexuality are a threat to the welfare of students who are assumed to be "born gay." This is so often the case with politically correct "conventional wisdom," exactly the reverse is true. Objections to homosexual behavior actually save lives and improve mental and physical health.

By posing as a part of the civil rights movement, homosexual activists have succeeded in attaching their message to the message of "human rights" and "tolerance" already incorporated into countless lessons in a typical curriculum, e.g., in social studies and literature classes. Homosexual advocacy takes the idea of being kind and civil and perverts it. Homosexuals, bisexuals and cross-gender practitioners are falsely alleged to be illegitimately discriminated against, even "oppressed" by the majority.

A "safe school" becomes one that doesn't threaten the "homosexual" student with disapproval. All students and staff are forced to stifle any objections to homosexual behavior or be vilified as "homophobes" and potential threats.

Propagandistic claims that "GLBT" students are at higher risk of suicide and are often the targets of bullies. They brow-beat school boards into accepting homosexual clubs, "anti-harassment" policies and tolerance programs. The truth is that many students are targets of bullies and not all of them demand a totalitarian regime of mental re-programming of their classmates to stop this. The reality is that the behaviors involved in homosexuality are the real risk to these children.]

Miracle 22

Andy

Jesus is my Lawyer

My little children, these things write I unto you, that ye sin not. And if any man sin, we have an advocate with the Father, Jesus Christ the righteous.(1 John 2:1)

"You need a lawyer," the Judge responded. I replied by saying, "Jesus is my lawyer." The Judge smirked and said, "Don't you know you are facing a fifty-year sentence?" With my body shaking I said, "Your honor, I am not the same person that I was once was. I have been 'born-again.'"

I was guilty of everything they had on my rap sheet and could have easily been sentenced to fifty years in prison. In fact, all those who went before the Judge that day got heavy sentences. The District Attorney wanted the Judge to throw the book at me as well. My serious charges included smuggling, conspiracy, illegal firearm sales, heavy weapons, drugs, and much more. I was considered a habitual criminal, with no hope for reform, and a misfit to society.

The Lord had graciously saved me a few months before this court date, a direct result of many prayers that my mother and wife had prayed for me for a very long time. I was on a downward spiral to hell. In fact, I thought that hell was my final destiny and I might as well live it up while alive and suffer the consequences later. I had done so many things that God could not forgive me for, I thought, so why bother Him. Of course I didn't understand the love and mercy of God. The ladies in my life finally lured me to church one night. I had made up my mind that I was not going to yield to the sway of man or beast. I was not going to change my ways. But, as soon as I stepped into the church, I began to weep uncontrollably. I was embarrassed and tried to hide my emotions. But the Lord had set the hook and I was caught. I prayed for the first time. Something came over me and I felt so clean. Why had I waited so long to find this marvelous truth?

Later I found the answer in the Bible. "But if our gospel be hid, it is hid to them that are lost: In whom the god of this world hath blinded the minds of them which believe not, lest the light of the glorious gospel of Christ, who is the image of God, should shine unto them" (2 Corinthians 4:3). The "god of this world" is the devil. He had blinded my mind and millions of others about the good news of Jesus Christ.

I was so excited about church that I didn't want to leave the building. The pastor hired me as janitor and this allowed me to be in God's house every day. I grew daily in prayer and Bible reading. But, I was still concerned about the court date that was hanging over my head.

My wife and my mother told me to let Jesus handle my case. They quoted "…we have an advocate with the Father, Jesus Christ the righteous" (1 John 2:1). They said, "Let Jesus be your lawyer and believe that He will set you free." That was easy for them to say, but it was not them facing the long prison sentence. But as a new Christian, God had already done miraculous things in my life. And for some strange reason I felt like He was going to get me out of this jam as well.

My knees smote one against the other as I stood before the bench. I knew that the next words I would hear from the court would determine my address for the rest of my natural life. "Did I really have enough faith that Jesus Christ loved me enough, a reformed sinner, to intercede for me?" I knew for sure that I was not worthy of such love.

The Judge said, "Tell me again, why you don't think you need a lawyer?" I told him, "Your honor, I believe you are a righteous judge and that you will make a just decision in my case." He squirmed around for a few seconds, that seemed like an eternity, and said, "I don't know why I am doing this but I decree you a four-year probated sentence. And I better not see you before my court again!" God, in His mercy, had performed a supernatural favor for me again. I was set free from sin and jail. It does not get much better than that.

For a while I thought that I had to go through my wife and mother to get to God. But, as they explained, Jesus was my personal Savior as well. This opened a direct line of communication between God and me. I could tell Him every need and He would respond. Prayer seemed to just flow through my mind.

I wanted to do more work for God, especially among the prison population. I was introduced to Kenneth Copeland Ministries who has an enormous prison ministry covering most of the United States. After sharing my burden with him, he placed me in charge of a large segment of that ministry. Now I get to witness for Jesus to inmates across the nation. We let the inmates know that they are more than just a number. They can become children of the King!

As you can tell by my testimony the devil tried to have me concealed for life, but the Lord intervened, and I have never been happier. My wife and I are seeing many souls added to the Kingdom of God.

Andy

Miracle 23

Alex
Minister in the Nation of Islam

My people are destroyed for lack of knowledge…. (Hosea 4:6)

I had been raised as a Christian in a predominately white church. My mother attended church, but my father did not. I learned many Bible stories in Sunday school and was taught that Jesus died for my sins. I can remember asking God to come into my heart, yet I never knew Him as my personal Savior. I liked going to church because it was a place to have fun and it gave me opportunities that other kids in my community did not have. People in the church were very loving and kind.

Each summer I looked forward to going to camp, which was sponsored by the Salvation Army. However, around the age of ten, I experienced both name-calling and sexual abuse from a counselor. This made me very angry.

When I was 15, four white boys attacked me and started kicking and stomping my body. My teacher, who was white, just stood there and watched them batter me. In self-defense I pulled a razor out of my pocket that I carried for protection.

The teacher called the police. I was charged with assault and battery and for carrying a concealed weapon. They took me to the juvenile section of the county jail and locked me up for three weeks.

"N----r, do you see this black jack? I am going to teach you a lesson." I was told to take off all my clothes, but I refused. After arguing and being threatened, I decided to comply, except for taking off my underwear. I was then thrown into a ten-foot by ten-foot metal box called "The Hole." It was cold and there was no light except for what was shining through a tiny peephole.

Shortly after being released from the juvenile center, I moved to Queens, New York to live with two of my aunts. It was during this time that I came in contact with the Muslims of the Nation of Islam. The only thing I knew about the Nation of Islam was what I had read in the autobiography of Malcolm X. He had lived in the East Elmhurst section of Queens, not far from where I lived. I noticed how clean the Muslims looked and how well they took care of business.

Because of drug use I ended up in a detention house called the Tombs and eventually was sent to prison. This is where I got involved with an Islamic group and eventually joined the Nation of Islam. The Nation of Islam offered me the moral teachings, discipline and direction that I needed, or so I thought.

After my release from prison, I moved back to New Jersey and got very involved in the Nation of Islam there. I started teaching the message of Elijah Muhammad in schools, jails, and community centers.

I went to Chicago to visit Elijah Muhammad. I also attended classes in Harlem, New York at Temple Number Seven. I met with Minister Louis Farrakan, who was the National Representative of the Honorable Elijah Muhammad. I learned all the lessons in the Nation of Islam that I could. I started reading the Koran and other Islamic books. I found out that these books did not coincide with some of the teachings of Mr. Muhammad.

I read the entire Koran and any book about Islam that I could find. Since no Muslim can pray properly in English, I learned to say my prayers in Arabic. I began to travel and study intensively in Egypt, Saudi Arabia, and Nigeria.

Because of my study, I eventually obtained the position of an IMAN (Inner-City Muslim Action Network). I delivered sermons in the mosque, led congregational prayers, and taught Islam on college campuses, in schools, and in communities. I began preaching very strongly against Christianity.

My twin sister was attending a Christian school called Christ for the Nations in Dallas, Texas. She wrote her views about Jesus Christ and I would respond about my belief. Once I wrote that Jesus could not have died on the cross. No one would die for others; it must have been suicide. She told me, "Regardless of what you say or believe, Jesus died for your sins and He loves you. Someday you are going to accept Christ and become a Christian." I responded, "Not in a million years."

My sister phoned me and said, "I have been praying for you. I challenge you to pray and ask God to prove to you that Jesus Christ is the Son of God and that He died on the cross for your sins." I accepted the challenge, because I was confident in Islam. I decided that if God would prove to me that Christ died for my sins, then I would become a Christian. If not, I would teach and promote Islam like never before.

One evening I was standing in front of a 7-11 store and suddenly a man asked me for directions to a church. When I asked him whom he knew in that church, he named my oldest sister. Realizing who I was, he said, "Oh, you are that Muslim we've been praying for." I insisted, "You don't have to pray for me. Islam is my religion. Allah is my god." Then a strange feeling came over me.

I kept challenging God with my prayers and strange things began to happen. One Sunday, after my teaching in the mosque on the story of Christmas and the Christian belief, a Muslim sister asked me to explain the Islamic view of the birth of Christ. I recited Surah 3:45-47 from the Koran. I had recited and explained these verses many times and had heard Islamic scholars explain them. Yet, as I spoke, for some unknown reason, doubt arose in my heart for the first time.

I was not sure of my answer. I began to intensify my study of the Bible, comparing references to Jesus in the Bible with the ones in the Koran. I had no problems with the teaching of the virgin birth. The Koran says in Surah 3:47, "She said, O my Lord, how shall I have a son, when no man hath touched me." (Translation by A. Yusuf Ali.) What Islam faith rejects is calling Jesus Christ the Son of God.

As an IMAM I lead prayers many times in Arabic. The recitation of the Koran is supposed to be word for word, without even one word left out. But for some reason I could not recite word for word any longer. I could hear a Muslim brother say, "Brother, because of your error of omitting a single word, Allah will not accept our prayers, and everyone's prayers are rejected." His words rang in my ears, and the weight of the responsibility was too great for me to bear. I told him that I would never lead prayer in the mosque again.

My sister invited me to attend her graduation at Christ for the Nations Bible School. I called her and said, "I believe this trip will be a turning point in my life. I have been praying that prayer you asked me to pray. When I come back I will either be a Christian, or I will rededicate my life to Islam."

Singing and praises filled the air at the graduation ceremony. I could sense something special. My sister introduced me to a former Muslim from Africa. He explained why he had become a Christian. He shared an awesome testimony of how he came to know Jesus Christ.

She also introduced me to an Egyptian student who was a former Muslim. I will never forget him. I was really impressed because he came from a long line of Muslims. He knew Islam and the Koran and was fluent in Arabic. He explained to me how God loved us so much that He came, Himself, in the very person of Jesus Christ to die on the cross for our sins. He left His high throne to take on human form and became a servant for mankind.

He told me that God was a personal God. He said his mother told him, "If you denounce Christianity, I will give you one million dollars. For you to confess that Jesus Christ is the Son of God is shirk [idolatry] in Islam." She said, "Son, if you do not denounce Christianity, then from this day forward you are no longer my son. You are dead." He told his mother that he could never, never deny Jesus Christ, because Jesus was his Savior. He told me he cried and was deeply hurt because his whole family turned their backs on him. His words touched my heart deeply.

I went to church with my sister. While the church folks were praising and worshipping God, I decided that I would give my life to Jesus Christ.

I did not understand what I had done, but I knew I was a changed man inside. It was like a heavy weight had been lifted off of me. I know that it is by God's grace that I am saved.

Albert Puig
Divorce Cancelled

I cried with my whole heart; hear me, O LORD: I will keep thy statutes.
(Psalm 119:145)

As I was seated at my desk alone one night I heard my mother and my friend Ron praying for me. Their prayer was just as clear as if they were in the same room. This really got my attention, because they were many miles away. While they were praying, I was out of my mind on cocaine, but God, in His infinite wisdom, mercy and grace was redirecting my life.

Up until this time in my life, I did basically whatever I wanted to do with no consideration for anything or anyone. I was my own worst enemy and could not stand success. I had everything a man could want, a faithful wife, healthy children, a house, cars and gainful employment, yet I felt empty. By using cocaine and marijuana, I tried to fill the big empty hole in my life; instead, I hurt and tried to destroy everything that I loved and was close to.

My wife, Patricia, whom I loved very much, was tired of the abuses and the insecurities associated with drug abuse. We separated on more than one occasion, each time due to drug abuse and increasing violence. She filed for divorce just months after the birth of our daughter, Elena. I broke her heart, spirit, and dreams with empty promises to change. Needless to say, she was devastated. Her departure from my life caused me to think and pray for help from Almighty God. I missed her, Brea and the baby and wanted them to come home. All I could think about was them coming home. I had managed to push away from me the ones that I loved and the ones that really loved me. The house was empty, and I grew worse in the weeks and months that lay ahead.

A few months later I received a call from Ron the same man that sold me a car and told me about Jesus Christ a few years earlier. This man of God (car salesman) had explained the gospel to me in such a way that I BELIEVED. Within minutes, after first meeting this fellow, he inquired about my relationship with Jesus. I began to ask questions and he supplied the Bible answers. In fact, that same day I repented of my sins before God and was re-baptized by immersion in the name of the Lord Jesus Christ.

Several years later he contacted me, shortly after my separation from my wife, and asked how things were going for me. I informed him that things were not so good for me at that time. He asked me if I wanted to go to church and I said yes but…I had not yet overcome my old habits.

After receiving the letter of divorce, I realized the chances of seeing my wife and children were getting worse. I tried many times and different ways to contact her over the next year, but she would not respond to me in any way, shape or form. It was here that I had to decide whether to continue on the old course or to chart a new one.

Ron started teaching me a series of Bible studies that completely changed my life. He proved to me that the Holy Spirit is for all men today and that His power would give me the strength to overcome all obstacles. I prayed for help and the Lord graciously filled me with His Spirit. I spoke in tongues just like countless others in the Bible have. I felt, for the first time, that I could make it without the drugs with God's help. My soul (heart, will and emotions) was filled with the

Spirit of God (love, peace, and joy) and I was no longer dependent on anything but Jesus Christ.

A few months later, my wife called me one afternoon (to my great surprise); she asked me, "Do you want to see the baby?"

He restored our hopeless marriage and my wife and children came home. Patricia and I dedicated our lives and our family to the Lord. We started attending church and Bible studies together. Since our reunion we have been blessed with two more daughters, Martha and Maria. All of us have been baptized and received the baptism of the Holy Spirit. God saved me, my wife, my children, and our family.

Life is good but Jesus Christ makes it great.

Albert

Miracle 25

Ian

Death on the Beach

Yea, though I walk through the valley of the shadow of death, I will fear no evil. (Psalm 23:4)

One night while I was diving for lobster on the small island of Mauritius I was stung on my forearm by five Box Jellyfish. A sting from a Box Jellyfish often proves to be fatal. Over seventy people have died from the stings. Many books quote this particular type of jellyfish to be among the most venomous creatures in the world.

By the time an ambulance arrived, my body was totally paralyzed and necrosis had begun to set into my bone marrow. En route to the hospital I began to see my life flash before my eyes. At this point in my life I was an atheist. I knew that I was nearly dead and didn't know if there was life after death. As I lay there dying, I saw my mother in a vision praying for me. She was encouraging me to cry out to God from my heart for help and He would hear and forgive me (my mother was the only Christian in our family). I didn't know what to pray so I cried out that if God was real, could He help me to pray? Immediately God showed me the Lord's prayer. For the first time in my life, I prayed from my heart and gave my life to the Lord.

When I arrived at the hospital the nurse took my blood pressure twice but could not find a pulse since my veins had collapsed. The doctors tried to save my life by injecting anti-toxins and dextrose into my body but seemingly to no avail. Within a few minutes I seemed to slip away from my body and my life stopped. I was dead. During this time I found myself in a very dark place. I tried to find a light switch, thinking I was still in the hospital, but as I reached out into the dark I couldn't touch anything. When I tried to touch my face my hand would go straight through my skull. Everything seemed so bizarre. I knew I was standing there but couldn't touch any part of my physical body. I could feel a cold eerie feeling as though something or someone was looking at me. I was in a spiritual darkness. From the darkness I began to hear men's voices screaming at me telling me to, "Shut up you are in hell, and you deserve to be here."

I couldn't believe what was happening. Then a radiant beam of light shone through the darkness and immediately began to lift me upward. I found myself being tranported up into an incredibly brilliant beam of pure white light. It seemed to be emanating from a circular opening far above me. I felt like a speck of dust being drawn up into this beam of light. I entered this opening to find myself inside a long narrow passageway or tunnel. At the far end of the tunnel I could see the source of the light. It was so radiant that it looked to be the center of the universe. As I continued to look toward this light, it seemed to draw me toward it at an incredible speed. I wasn't walking but was being transported along this tunnel toward the source of this light. I watched as a wave of light broke off the source and moved up the tunnel towards me. As it passed through me I could feel a wave of warmth and comfort flood my soul. It was incredible. This light wasn't just physical but was giving off a living emotion. Coming out of the end of this tunnel I found myself standing in the presence of an awesome light and power. It seemed as though the constellations in the universe must find their energy source from this focal point.

I stood there and wondered to myself if this was just an energy source in the universe or if perhaps there could be someone standing in the midst of this light? A voice immediately responded to my thought and asked me, "Ian, do you wish to return?"

"Return," I thought! "Where am I?" As I looked over my shoulder I could see the tunnel going back into darkness. "Darkness and hospital bed, am I out of my body? Is this real, am I standing here? Or am I in a coma having some bizarre dream?"

As I looked back toward the light, it was still there and I responded, "I don't know where I am, but if I am out of my physical body I wish to return." The voice responded, "If you wish to return you must see in a new light." "New light," I thought, "I'm seeing the light." "Are you the true light?" Words appeared in front of me, "God is light and in Him is no darkness at all (1 John 1:5)." I had never read a Bible before in my life so I didn't know this was straight out of the Scriptures. "God is light," I thought. "This is pure light. I see no darkness. I have just come from darkness. I see no evil. Am I standing in the presence of God? He knows my name and I didn't tell Him. Only God could do that. He knows what I am thinking before I even speak. Then he must be able to see everything I have done wrong in my life. No, I don't want God to see that." I felt totally exposed and wanted to move away from the light and go back into the darkness where I belonged. I thought someone had made a mistake and brought the wrong person before God.

As I drew back toward the darkness, a wave of light swept through me. I felt pure unadulterated love flow over me. "Love," I thought, "how could God love me? I've taken his name in vain. I'm not a good man." No matter what I said, waves of His unconditional love continued to flow over me. I found myself weeping uncontrollably in His Presence. It was so amazing that He had totally forgiven me and accepted me as I was.

The waves of love ceased and I wondered if I could possibly step into the light and see what God looked like. I was so close to Him. I asked if I could step in? I heard no response but thought, "If God could love me so much, He wouldn't mind." As I stepped into the light I found myself disappear into its brightness. It had the intensity of laser light, yet I could look directly at it. The light seemed to absorb me into it. The center seemed to be very bright so I aimed for it. I could feel a healing presence coming off this light that was healing my broken heart. It was touching me deep inside my heart of hearts where no one gets to see. It was so beautiful.

Suddenly it opened up in the center and standing in front of me was the most awesome sight imaginable. I could see a man standing in front of me, but He was not like anyone I'd ever seen before in my life. His garments were shimmering white in color and apparel of light. I could see His bare feet and His hands were outstretched toward me as if to welcome me. I knew I was looking upon God. As I looked toward His face the intensity of the light seemed to increase seven-fold. I could not make out the form of His face as the light was so bright. It was such purity, holiness, and beauty. I asked God if I could step closer. I felt I could. I wanted to see His face. Moving closer, waves of more love began to flow towards me, and I felt very safe. I was only a few feet away from the Lord. I tried to see His face. I didn't know that no man can see the face of God and live.

I moved my face into the radiance that surrounded His face. When He moved, all His Glory moved with Him. Directly behind Him was an opening to a new world with green pastures, a crystal clear stream, and rolling green hills. To my right, mountains were in the distance, and blue skies were above. To my left I saw fields interspersed with trees and flowers. As I looked at the grass in front of me I could see the same light that was on the presence of God was also radiating throughout this entire creation, totally untouched by man, a perfect creation. And in my heart I knew I belonged here, and that God had created me to live here. I knew I was home.

I was just about to enter in and explore, when God stepped back in front of me, and asked me this question. "Now that you have seen, do you wish to step in or do you wish to return?" I thought, "I don't want to return. I wish to step in." I have no one to go back for and no one has ever loved me. All they've ever done is manipulate me and try to control me. I have no one to go back for. "I wish to step in," I told God. But God didn't move. I looked back behind me to say, "Goodbye, cruel world." Standing behind me in a vision in front of the tunnel was my mother. As soon as I saw her I knew that there was one person in my life that had shown me love and that was my mother. She had prayed for me every day and tried to show me that this was the way. In my mind I thought, "If I am dead and I did choose to step into heaven, what would my mother think? Would she know I made it or would she think I went to Hell, because she knew I had no faith?" I realized that it could break her heart and that she would have no reason to believe that God had heard my prayer in the ambulance and forgiven my sins. I thought, "How can I do that to my mum, it would be so selfish?" I decided to return to my body.

God then spoke to me and said that if I wished to return, I must see things in a new light. I understood that to mean that I must begin to see through His eyes of love, peace, joy, and forgiveness.

Looking back toward the tunnel again I now could see a vision of all my family, and thousands and thousands of other people. I asked God, "Who are all these people?" He told me that if I didn't return many of these people would not get a chance to hear about Him.

I told God that I didn't know most of them and I didn't love them, but that I loved my mother and wished to return for her. God spoke to me and told me that He loved those people and wanted them all to come to know Him. I asked God how could I possibly return back down the tunnel and back into my hospital bed. He spoke and said, "Son, tilt your head. Now feel the liquid drain from your eye. Now open your eye and see." And I was immediately back in my physical body.

As I opened my eye, I was back on a hospital bed with my right leg elevated, and cupped in the hands of the young Indian doctor who had been trying to save my life. He had a scalpel or some sharp instrument in his hand and he was prodding the base of my foot like a dead piece of meat. He wasn't aware that I was looking at him. I thought, "What's that man doing with my foot? What is he doing with that knife?" At the same time something seemed to spook the doctor and he quickly turned his head to see my right eye open. I was looking at him. Terror struck his face and I got the distinct impression that he had just seen a dead man looking at him. My eye wasn't moving much. I could see the doctor thinking to himself that perhaps he had hit a nerve in my foot and caused the corpse to twitch. He thought that he had the evil eye looking at him or something.

As for me, I was trying to grapple with what I had just seen. Did I just see God? Has He just given my life back? As I lay there, I heard the voice of God say, "Son, I have just given you your life back." I said, "If that is true God, could you help me tilt my head to the left and look out of the other eye?" I was getting sick of looking at the doctor's terrified face. Strength came back into my neck and I opened my left eye. I saw a whole bunch of nurses and orderlies standing in the doorway looking at me as if the dead had just risen. As my eye locked onto theirs, they began to jump backwards out of the doorway. From what I can ascertain I had been dead for a period of some fifteen minutes. I prayed to God that night and asked him to heal me. The next day I walked out of the hospital completely healed.

I asked God, "What have I become?" I knew that my entire life was changing for the good. God told me I was a reborn Christian and that He wanted me to read His Bible. I had never read a Bible and had never heard about being "born-again." Over the next six weeks I read the entire Bible. I have never been the same since I saw our Lord Jesus Christ in His Glorified form.

Ian

Miracle 26

Ron Knott
Hungry Soul

…ye shall be witnesses…. (Acts 1:8)

"God lead me to a hungry soul," was my prayer. My pastor had challenged our church to pray that prayer and he promised that we would see God in action. I was shocked at how quickly my prayer was answered.

As an airline pilot, I traveled to many different cities every week. After several hours of flying our crew would layover, or spend the night, at a predetermined city. When I prayed that prayer I was in my hotel room in New Orleans.

A few hours after my prayer, which I had forgotten about, I decided to walk down to Canal Street for a cup of coffee. As I was walking toward the little coffee shop I passed a drunk lying in the ditch alongside the road. I thought, "What a waste of human life."

I ordered my coffee from the waiter and within seconds that old dirty drunk, that I had just passed, came and sat at the stool next to me. He smelled so bad that I could hardly drink my coffee. He looked at me with his bloodshot eyes and said, "Would you give me some money? I'm hungry." I said, "No, but I will buy you something to eat."

I ordered him a hamburger steak. The onions and gravy were piled high on his platter when he was served. In fact, he had the onions and gravy all over the counter, and me as well, as he was eating. He seemed to be in a semi-passed-out condition nodding back and forth.

All of a sudden, I felt an urge to witness to this drunkard. I said to myself, "This has got to be the wrong spirit. This poor fellow is in no state to listen to me." But, I started talking to him anyhow. I don't remember what I said other than, "Fellow you must have a praying mother because God wants me to talk with you. You need to get your life right with God." He did not respond.

After a few minutes of this torture, I paid for his food and my coffee and departed the café. I thought I had missed God by a million miles and I felt like a complete fool. But as I was leaving the restaurant, a young man followed me to the sidewalk. He stopped me and said, "Sir, what Gospel do you preach?" I said, "You must have me confused, I'm not a preacher." He said, "You thought you were witnessing to that wino in the restaurant, but you were talking directly to me." Wow!" My faith came alive.

He said, "My life has gone from bad to worse. The lady I was sitting with in the restaurant was not my wife. I lost my job and family because of drinking. The Lord has been giving me dreams of what is going to happen to me if I don't change my ways. Would you please pray with me?" "Of course, I will be glad to," I said. My faith was increased even more.

He said, "I had a good job with an airline and was fired because of drinking." I asked, "What airline?" He said, "Delta." That just happened to be the airline I was flying for. My faith increased again.

He said, "I was in a great church in Indianapolis, but have not attended in a long while." I asked, "What church?" He told me and I was again shocked because I knew the pastor.

I began to realize that God was answering my prayer for a hungry soul that day. We talked for a while and I gave him the name of a pastor I knew in New Orleans that would be eager to help him. I had to get back to the hotel and put on my uniform and get to the airport.

A year later, just before Christmas, I received a phone call from a man by the name of Ben Brown. He said, "Hi Ron. Do you remember me?" I said Mr. Brown do I know you from college, navy, or the airlines?" He said, "Do you remember witnessing to the wino about this time last year in New Orleans when in fact, the message was for me?" I said, "Yes, yes, yes, how could I ever forget that miracle! How are you doing?" He said, "I just called to thank you for being sensitive to the Spirit that day. I have my family back, my job back, and am in a wonderful church in Orlando, Florida."

I was the one blessed. I only prayed a simple prayer that day to be led to a hungry soul. God arranged all the impossible situations to get me to the backslider. Yet, I thought I was completely out of step with God .This again, proves to me that the greatest and most precious gift God can give us, after He has saved our soul, is another soul. One soul is worth more than the greatest gold find, the richest diamond mine, the most productive oil/gas lease and the greatest real-estate deal combined. One soul is worth more than the whole world! God wants to give us many of these high-praise items. You can have as many as you want. There is no limit. Souls are not an endangered species. They are all around us. Soul-winning is a great way to increase your eternal financial statement and your long-term retirement plan.

As we note in the Scriptures there is happiness in heaven when one sinner repents. "…I say to you, there is joy in the presence of the angels of God over one sinner that repents" (Luke 15:10 NKJV).

It is noted that the rich man wanted someone to tell his five brothers so that they would not come into the terrible place of torment. Then he said, "I beg you therefore, father, that you would send him to my father's house, for I have five brothers, that he may testify to them, lest they also come to this place of torment" (Luke 16:27-28 NKJV).

Not only do those who reside in Heaven want us to witness, those in hell and torment are screaming for someone to tell their loved ones before it is too late.

"Ye shall be witnesses" as recorded in Acts 1:8. The same word, shall, is recorded in Romans 10:9. How can we accept one shall and omit the other shall?

Ron Knott

Miracle 27

Ray

Holiness in Action

…that you bear much fruit, showing yourselves to be my disciples.
(John 15:8 NIV)

A friend told me that the Lord gave him the following vision during an early morning prayer meeting. He said, "I wanted to lead someone to Christ but had not been successful."

He said, "While I was in earnest prayer I felt as if I was traveling down a long road. The road forked. One fork went up over a high hill toward a bright light, the other fork went down a spiral path into darkness. I took the fork that went toward the bright light. As soon as I made that decision I felt like Jesus was by my side."

"We traveled to the top of the high mountain and could see a beautiful city just over the crest. The Lord led me to a large banquet hall. Inside this ravishing hall were many tables set for a large gathering. Each place setting had beautiful arrangements of china, silverware and napkin rings."

"The Lord led me to a long table that would seat scores of people. He showed me my name on the napkin ring at the head of one table. All other napkin rings at this table were blank. He said, 'This is your table; go and fill it.' I then told the Lord 'I would like to see what was on the other end of the road that lead to darkness." As he led me down the path toward darkness I saw people who were trapped along either side of the road. Their souls seemed to be asking for someone to come to their aid to help them out of this evil place. Their bodies seemed somewhat content in the pleasures there."

"I saw a large cliff with flames leaping up over the side. As I approached this horrifying place, I saw the old drunkard of my town struggling to hold on to the edge of the cliff. He was saying, 'SAVE ME, SAVE ME.' I told him I could not save him. The Lord said, 'You can save him if you try.'"

He said, "When the vision was over I was a changed man. I knew where this drunkard lay in the streets of my city. The very next Sunday morning I went after this old gentleman. I loaded his dirty, stinking body in my car and took him to church. The church members turned away from this unsightly man as we were seated on the back row. The pastor preached a message of love that morning. This old, forgotten man, made his way to an altar of repentance and gave his life to Jesus. I know the angels in heaven rejoiced that morning. But, the church members had a look of repulsion on their faces. The pastor took the old man out to lunch. He was given clean clothes and a chance to take a much-needed bath. That night the old drunkard told how happy and how thankful he was that someone cared. The next Wednesday night I went to the lumberyard, where he worked as a security guard, to take him to church. I was told that he had been killed that afternoon when a pile of lumber crushed him. I know I will have at least one person at my table. How many names do you have at your table?"

Friends, this is holiness in action. He was not interested in man made holiness, he was interested in Bible holiness. He is a disciple of Jesus, not a Christian political band.

Ray

William
Miracle Healing

I rejoice in awe of you and the miracles the Lord has performed.
(Dr. Dino Delaportas, MD)

Giving all the praise, honor and glory unto the Lord through whom this testimony is made possible this eleventh day of November 2000.

My physician, as evidenced in this document, has confirmed the miracles I received from the Lord during a Faith and Victory Service. The service was at the World Harvest Church with Pastor Rod Parsley delivering the Word on November 5th, 2000.

On Monday, May 13, 1985 I was involved in a motorcycle v. train accident which resulted in a closed head injury (massive traumatic brain injury), ruptured optic nerve (right eye), and spinal injuries. These injuries left me a quadriplegic (no use of my lower extremities and only partial use of my right hand with no feeling on my entire right side), cognitive deficits and short-term memory loss. As you can imagine, these injuries were tremendously life changing. However, being a "born-again" Christian, as well as having been an Emergency Medical Technician for several years before my accident, I was better situated in overcoming my injuries and moving forward with my life. Although I was confined to a wheelchair, I was able to continue through Him in my education at Salisbury State University, Hagerstown Junior College, and Prince George's Community College where I was a student in General Studies and Para-Legal Studies.

While attending Salisbury State University in 1987, I became involved in wheelchair sports and excelled in shooting. Over the next three years God blessed me with thirty-nine Gold Medals, fourteen Silver, and three Bronze and opportunities to compete in Regional, State, National, International, World Championships, and in the 1988 Paralympics in Seoul, South Korea. During this time God also blessed me with nineteen National and World Records.

In 1993, while attending Prince George's Community College, I was blessed in an internship with Judge William D. Missouri, the Administrative Judge of the Circuit Court for Prince George's County (the first such internship in the Para-Legal program).

During the time between 1994 and June 2000, I went through a lot of turmoil in both my personal and professional life and was separated in faith through choice and ignorance. I thought I knew better without the Lord; was I ever wrong. This was perhaps the most destructive time in my life. I attempted suicide twice, lost the love of my life (so I thought), lost a business, and lots of friends.

Finally in July 2000, due to circumstances beyond my control, I was stuck at my sister-in-Christ's house with a broken-down van. During this time I was lead back to the Lord and magnificent things started happening. I became so full of the Spirit that I lost control and completely surrendered unto Him. I became active in the church (The Tabernacle Church of Laurel, Maryland) and have been working on computers at the church since.

About three weeks before the November 5th service at the World Harvest Church, the Lord let me know that I needed to be in Columbus, Ohio on November 5th. I didn't know why. I didn't know anyone in Columbus, nor had I ever heard of Pastor Rod Parsley, or the World Harvest Church.

About two weeks later I saw an infomercial about a Debt Burning Service at the World Harvest Church in Columbus, Ohio. The Lord immediately impressed me to call the church and attend the church service that was to be held on November 5th.

On the evening of Thursday, November 2nd I told the folks at Tabernacle Church in Laurel, Maryland that I was to go to the World Harvest Church in Columbus, Ohio for my healing. I had several ailments. Pastor Gurley prayed over me for healing and took an offering to cover my expenses to Columbus. I would not have been able to make the trip without this financial blessing.

Upon arrival at the World Harvest Church, a 400-mile trip, I called the church and got the Prayer Line. As they prayed I felt a burning sensation in my feet. I knew that the Lord was at work in my body. I professed, through Him, that I would be healed.

During the service at the World Harvest Church on November 5th, Pastor Parsley called all those that needed healing to come forward. He named a lot of ailments and afflictions that the Lord would heal. I went to the front as many others did.

I could feel the Lord working on my body. As I was adjusting myself in my wheelchair one of the ushers asked if I was trying to get out of my chair. Before I had a chance to respond, the Spirit took control and spoke through me and said, "I'm going to jump out of this chair in thirty seconds." And in thirty seconds I was standing for the first time in fifteen years.

The usher then asked, "Can you walk?" I said, "I don't know." I took a few steps and he said, "Can you walk up the stairs?" I replied, "Let's ask the Lord!" The Lord helped me up those stairs to the platform.

Before I entered the World Harvest Church that evening, my blood sugar was 470. I had been without insulin for three days. After being prayed for my blood sugar dropped to 128 without medication. God had performed another miracle in my body.

When I returned home my pastor allowed me to give my testimony in the church. Many were blessed and healed that night.

The Lord let me know that many others would have their faith increased and be healed in hearing testimonies such as mine.

Be blessed and relax in the Spirit of the Lord. He is an awesome God and I am thankful he healed me and is still in the healing business. It is my desire to take this message around the world for my Lord and Savior, Jesus Christ.

William

Dad

Deathbed Salvation

And when they came that were hired about the eleventh hour, they received every man a penny. (Matthew 20:9)

A few years ago, one Thursday night, the Lord impressed me to go visit my parents who lived about 300 miles from my home. My wife and I had not planned to visit them for a couple more weeks. I had talked with them a few days before and everything seemed to be going fine. In fact, my dad had just had a complete physical and the doctors gave him a clean bill of health. But something told me that I needed to go there immediately. So my wife and I headed for my hometown in Louisiana.

When we arrived at my parent's home, we discovered that my dad was a very sick man. He didn't know what was wrong. Neither did the doctors. All we knew was that dad was in the local hospital. He was in severe pain.

Dad hardly ever went to church. He would go to weddings and funerals and that was about it. But my mother was a faithful saint if there ever was one. Dad had been the mayor of our city for years. He was a big man in statue and reputation. He worked hard and expected everyone who worked for him to work hard as well. He was a good-hearted individual and helped a lot of people who could not help themselves. I can remember many times that he would get up after midnight and drive sick folks to the nearest hospital which was miles away. But when questioned about going to church he would say, "I am as good as the church folks. In fact a lot of them work for me and they are crooks." And he had been swindled by a group of Christians so he had very little respect for most of them.

As a matter of fact, I didn't go to church much either. I was a Navy pilot and an airline pilot and church just did not mix with my lifestyle. But the Lord had gotten my attention a few months earlier and I had completely surrendered my life to Him.

Dad saw the great change in my lifestyle. And when I would visit him he would go to Sunday school with me, but he never made a commitment to the Lord. Of course, we were all happy that he had made a start. My mother had prayed for his salvation for more than 40 years and she was not about to let up one bit.

My faith for Dad to come to the Lord was severely tested. But, when I saw how sick he was, I made a final plea for him to ask the Lord to forgive him and save his soul. "Dad, God has got you in this situation for a purpose and I want to pray for you," I said. My mother, my wife, and I laid our hands on him and asked the Lord to heal him and save his soul. Then he began to pray. In just a few moments he was speaking in a heavenly language. A beautiful glow came upon his face and he said, "I have never felt happier in my whole life. Praise the Lord!" We were so thrilled. Dad also said, "Son, I did this because of you." In other words he saw a real change in me after I became a Christian. Little did I know that he was observing my new life. Up to that time I thought that my witnessing to him was in vain. Dad had taken in every word and action that he noticed in my new Christian life and carefully considered the entire situation.

Dad continued to get worse. He was getting sicker by the hour. I kept the trail hot to the little chapel in the hospital praying for him. As a young Christian I was not very familiar with the Scriptures. But more than once I would flip open my Bible and it would stop at

John 14:13-14 which says, "And whatsoever ye shall ask in my name, that will I do, that the Father may be glorified in the Son. If ye ask any thing in my name I will do it." I was more interested in the Lord saving his soul than healing his body and that is the way I prayed.

Three days later, we had Dad's funeral. The funeral was like a revival. Yes, we were very sad, heart broken, and missed him very much. Yet we were happy that God had mercifully saved him at the last hour. They discovered, after his death, that he had cancer of the liver and it took him out in less than one week. God had answered my mother's many prayers to save his soul; what better could we ask for?

I must say the old enemy started to work on me soon after the funeral. He kept putting thoughts in my mind like, "He didn't really get saved. He didn't do anything for God so how could you expect him to be saved?" I soon had enough of those impressions and asked the Lord to show me somehow if my dad was really saved.

In a very short time, I had three dreams about Dad. In the first two dreams I saw him standing up singing and worshiping the Lord in the church. He looked great and had a big smile on his face. The third dream was somewhat different and really got my attention. I dreamed that Dad was in a morgue and was about to be embalmed. In this dream I knew that he was not dead and they were about to drain the blood from his body, which would kill him for sure. I was struggling, like you do sometimes in a dream, trying to get to him before it was too late. Finally, I reached him just seconds before they placed him on the table for embalming. I screamed, "He is not dead!" I took him by the hand and he raised up. The next scene in the dream was that he was in the church singing with a big smile on his face.

I believe the Lord let me have those dreams to show me to never give up on anyone. I had reached Dad just in time. I am thankful that the Lord impressed me to go to his home. I am thankful that I went. I am thankful that we were able to pray with him. I am thankful that the Lord saved him on the one-yard line of hell.

Never give up on your dad, mother, sister, son, daughter, brother, friend or foe, stranger, or anyone else. They may be watching you as Dad was watching me. This could be your best testimony—or your worst.

Ron

Miracle 30

Sherry
From Darkness to Light

Thou shalt have no other gods before me. (Exodus 20)

My mother and stepfather consulted mediums. Sometimes they would take me to a seance. They loved to talk about the thrills of their astral projections (out of body experiences) and the power of the mind. My brother and I were fascinated by all they told us. It seemed that the more they became involved in their quest to become "higher beings", the more my parents became abusive, distrustful and delusional.

The mediums often spoke of the spirits that surrounded and accompanied my parents, who were proclaimed by the spirits as a "psychic healer".

Apparently, these "spirit guides" attached themselves to my parents and followed them home after the meetings. You could actually feel their presence, and strange things kept happening, like doorknobs would move when no one was near them. Sometimes our cats would follow something around and meow at it. My brother and I were really scared when this happened but my parents always laughed, insisting that they were friendly spirits or at worst mischievous.

I knew nothing of Jesus except what the spiritualists taught. However, I went with a friend to a revival where I head the gospel for the first time. What the preacher said scared me enough that I went to the altar and sincerely prayed the sinner's prayer. As I knelt there, I felt the sweet touch of a different spirit, but I didn't know then that it was my first encounter with God's Holy Spirit. I was baptized that night. I hid our baptismal certificates from Mom because I knew she would be furious. Sure enough, when she did find out I believed in God, she overwhelmed me with questions far beyond my ability to answer. Mostly out of self-defense, I abandoned my new faith. My mother also made me say I did not believe in the Holy Spirit.

When I was twelve, I began to see what the mediums saw in the spiritual realm, even at home! My parents were very excited, telling me that if I chose to, I could become a very powerful medium and help many people. With encouragement, I explored hypnotism, ESP, numerology, palm-reading, and auras. Eventually, I decided to concentrate my studies on astrology and white witchcraft, which is the practice of removing a hex, or curse, or invoking good fortune on someone. I was very interested in helping people.

One morning I woke up filled with an overwhelming appreciation for God's creation, even though I no longer believed in God. This was not my usual angry state of mind, and I wondered at the joy and peace I felt. As I tried to get out of bed, an invisible hand pushed me back. Suddenly I saw the incredibly beautiful underside of a white dove, made completely of light, flying by at great speed. A quiet voice in my mind whispered, "Father, Son, Holy Spirit." I knew the vision was from heaven, but I honestly had no idea what the words meant. Later that summer when I attended a Catholic church with my maternal grandmother and heard the same phrase, I at least understood that it had something to do with the Bible.

My stepfather's mother was a "black witch", and he firmly believed she was determined to destroy him. Thoroughly frightened, he rallied his family behind him to "return her hexes" (a white witch tactic), explaining to us that he was weary of her curses. She soon became ill, and sent me a letter telling me that I was "her favorite."

The night she died, I was awakened from a dream with a very loud knock on my bedroom door. In the dream I had seen a picture of Jesus at a door, knocking, and had been told, "The devil knocks, too. Don't let him in." The knock was so loud that my parents heard it too, but acted unconcerned.

That same night, I felt a cold chill enter my room and witnessed objects move around. This "poltergeist" remained in my room for the next few years. It was easy for me to deduce that it was related to my step-grandmother, since my stepfather told me later how she had tormented him with her spirits late at night: "I used to be terrified at the knocks in my room. And I could hear laughing down the hall. But that's just how the spirits announce themselves. We hear it in seances." Because of their earlier reactions to such things, I didn't report the ghost.

I decided that there had to be a God. My conclusion was based solely on logic. I realized nothing but an omniscient Creator could devise the intricate perfection of natural phenomena (mysteries we humans have not yet been able to decipher). Random chance could not explain these things. I was learning the truth of the passage in Scripture that says, "For since the creation of the world His invisible attributes, His eternal power and divine nature, have been clearly seen, being understood through what has been made…."

When I was fifteen I thought it would be fun to use my powers on a boy at school to make him become my boyfriend. Even as I did it, I felt ashamed for trying to control someone. Wavering between spiritualism and Christianity, I prayed for God's forgiveness. I sincerely asked Him to show himself to me.

Not more than fifteen minutes later, I met a Pentecostal girl who listened to me mouth off on the powers of Jeanne Dixon. When she asked me if I had ever heard of the Holy Spirit, I almost fell over!

Miraculously, Mom let me spend the night with this total stranger. When I did tell her about the church, she seemed happy I was exploring "new power." My friend was a sincere and loving Christian. I challenged every statement she made about the Bible; I often shouted at her that I didn't want to hear that nonsense, but she remained patient and did not reject me.

When I stayed with her and went to that Pentecostal church, I would be tormented by migraine headaches. Loud, fast-talking voices would come into my mind, arguing against the existence of God. The voice would repeat the teachings of spiritualism.

At first I thought it was just my own mind reacting to the confusion inside, but as I began to argue with that voice, I realized it could not be my own thoughts. I remembered the vision from heaven and the other gentle voice whispering, "Father, Son, Holy Spirit," and I thought hard about the possibility that Jesus was more than just a great teacher.

The more I attended the church meetings, the more I became convinced that I was in the middle of a spiritual battle. I realized I had to make a choice between the powers of darkness and the light of God.

Just before one of the meetings, I made my decision. As I sat there preparing myself for this step of faith, I heard singing. It sounded like a choir of thousands praising God with the most beautiful song I had ever heard. I looked around to see who was making that beautiful music. No one else in the room could hear it. It became clear to me that I was hearing angels sing.

With joy in my heart, I went forward to the altar and asked to be prayed for. I told them I wanted to be delivered from the demon that harassed me, and that I wanted to be baptized in the Holy Spirit. As they prayed over me, I was filled again with God's Holy Spirit and completely released from a spirit of witchcraft. That night, I could even read a King James Bible, and understand it easily! My previous difficulty in understanding the Bible was gone.

Of course, my parents were furious. They attacked me. Their hatred and paranoia seemed to know no bounds. They were convinced that my Christian friends and I were praying down hexes on them. They refused to allow me to see them or talk with my Christian friends for more than six months. I was a virtual prisoner in their house.

I was careful never to preach to them. In fact, I avoided them as much as possible, but they went out of their way to provoke a confrontation. They would ask me a question, then blow up when I answered. Some rages lasted for up to five hours.

Mom was angry because the spirits complained to her that they could no longer get into my room. So she burned my Christian books and hid my Bible, forcing me to read their books instead. She chose to ignore her own vision of the "dove" only the week before. She refused to believe it was the Holy Spirit. God enveloped me with a new strength and love that was not my own. As he continued to sustain me, I was reminded of the apostle Paul's encouraging words to Timothy: "God has not given us a spirit of fear, but of power and love and a sound mind." Unfortunately, expressions of love to my parents only made them even further enraged and frightened.

My parents moved to California and I stayed with my dad. My stepfather lost large sums of money because he placed bets on UFO landings.

The New Age Movement is nothing new. It falsely teaches that we are gods within ourselves and can control our own destinies, and this is what attracts people to it. Many rely on spirits for advice on every facet of life. I know from experience that these are lying spirits who do not have our best interests at heart! Similarly, Christians rely on God for advice, but the similarity ends there. I also know from experience that God does have our best interests at heart.

We are created in the image of God, and our greatest power is the God-ordained power of choice. We have the power to choose between good and evil, allegiance to God or to Satan, eternal life or death. He gave us the freedom to reject Him, even though He never rejects us when we seek Him sincerely and with humility.

It has been almost twenty years since I decided to turn to God's ways instead of Satan's lies, a decision I have never regretted. I began a whole new life of light when I accepted Jesus and dedicated my life to him. He has healed my mind of the terrible damage done by my parents and the occult. He has replaced hatred with love and turned my sorrows into joy. God has given me a sound mind, just as he promised he would.

It is because of God's love for you that I write this account for you, exposing the pain of my past for the sake of your soul. I have played with the fires of New Age and have been burned. But I am thankful that I stumbled in the darkness and have known true evil so that I could recognize the true light, which is Jesus. God himself says, "They that diligently seek Me shall find Me." How about you? Will you be a friend of God, or will you get lost in the twisted maze of the New Age, and lose your soul in exchange for so little while you search for that elusive "new truth" just around the corner?

Jesus Christ said in John 14:6 "I am the way, the truth, and the life: no man cometh unto the Father, but by me."

Sherry

Sharon

The Beauty of Death

Precious in the sight of the LORD is the death of his saints.
(Psalm 116:15)

I felt Mom's spirit flow through my hand the moment she died. It was such a wonderful and peaceful experience and something I will always cherish.

Although she was my mother-in-law we could not have been closer. She loved me and I loved her. She lived in our home the last seventeen years of her life and was a great comfort to me while my husband was out of town. He was an airline pilot and was gone frequently.

During our time together, I noted that she would get calls from all across the country with prayer requests. When folks had a real need, they called mom for prayer. They knew she was an extraordinary prayer warrior and she would, in fact, take their request before the throne of God and not just give them lip service.

She was such a sweet lady and the love of her life was her Lord Jesus. She prayed and read her Bible daily and was such a blessing to have around. Many times she would say, "I prayed all last night because the Lord gave me a burden to intercede for this person." She spent a lot of time in intercessory prayer.

This dreadful night the family had been called in and was told that mom only had a few hours to live. She had been in fairly good health during her ninety-six years. However the last two years of her life, she was not able to walk although her mind was as clear as ever. Then she had a stroke that took away much of her ability to function. She had always made the family promise that we would not prolong her passing by artificial means.

The family was in her room that final night, watching her struggling for every breath. This was such a horrible experience. We knew it would be just a short time until she died. We gathered around her bed and my husband prayed for the Lord to take her. He said, "Lord we thank you for our mother of ninety-six years. Now she is in such pain and discomfort. Would you please take her on to heaven and not prolong her sickness?"

I had my hand on mom's chest as he prayed for the Lord to take her home. I had asked the Lord, many times, to give me a vision, dream, or some indication of mom's soul departing when she died. I really wanted to see her angel in the room with her. After the short prayer my husband turned and walked only about one step from her bedside. Within seconds I felt mom's spirit flow through my hand. It was such a wonderful and peaceful feeling. I said, "She is gone!" No one in the room had noticed that mom had passed but me. Her spirit departed through my hand and on to glory. The nurse was called and she confirmed that mom had died. This bitter-sweet experience let me know that the Lord called her home at the right time.

A few days later my husband was thanking God for allowing his mother to live ninety-six years. He told mom that we loved her and missed her very much. Instantly, there came a reply. He heard mom's voice say, "Everything is going to be all right, son!" He did not expect her to reply. He had not asked that she reply. There is no way he could have mimicked mom's voice. The Lord let him know where mom was and that she knew what was happening on the earth. And, in a short time, everything turned out all right just as mom said it would. Of course this brought rivers of tears to his eyes. The Lord is so good.

Mom's funeral was like a revival. People from far and near told how she had ministered to them in years past. My husband wrote the following poem in remembrance of his mom.

Grandma's Testimony

Please don't stand at my grave and cry,
For I am not here—I did not die.

The angels transported me in one big leap,
I am now at peace at Jesus' feet.

It's so great to see my old friends—and kin,
Who will never be old again.

They embraced me and welcomed me in,
I am not dead; I am more alive than I have ever been.

Jesus had a record of all those I had prayed for and fed,
He provided for my sin—and theirs—when He bled!

Don't stand at my grave and cry,
I am not there; I did not die.
                                            Ron Knott

Sharon

155